BRAUGHING LOCAL HISTO

Braughing at War Se

CW00573556

THE LAST POST

BY PETER BOYLAN

First published 2014
Copyright: text © Braughing Local History Society 2014
Photographs © Braughing Local History Society and individual owners
All rights reserved

ISBN 978-0-9546901-3-7

Published by
Braughing Local History Society
The Gables
Green End
Braughing
Ware
Hertfordshire SG11 2PG

Typesetting and origination Madeline and Clive Marshall

Printed in Great Britain by
www.czdesignandprint.co.uk

CONTENTS

The Longman family in the garden at Upp Hall on 15th July 1905. Left to right: Charles, Sibyl, William, Mary, Freddy and Harriet

FOREWORD

This War is a beastly business - wrote Freddy Longman to his parents just weeks before he was killed on 18th October, 1914.

To grasp the atrocity of the numbers of people killed during the First World War is impossible. By concentrating on one person, Peter Boylan has given us an insight into that vast tragedy which unfolded one hundred years ago. And anyone who has lost a loved young person will empathise with the devastating grief Freddy's death brought to his parents, siblings and friends; a grief that was replicated millions of times.

We are extremely fortunate that Freddy's family kept so much material – his war diary; letters from the battlefield; photographs; and paintings. They have generously allowed Peter Boylan access to them. During the past few years Peter has worked tirelessly on this material and has researched Freddy's earlier life.

The result of his work is a rounded picture of an extraordinary and gifted young man. In many ways, he is the epitome of the English hero. Freddy was a keen sportsman and happy in his chosen military life; but he was also a talented artist; he cared about what the war was doing to the people and landscape of France and Belgium; he looked after his platoon making sure they were fed and cared for, right down to the socks they wore. In return he engendered respect and loyalty.

After reading this account we will surely say "What a waste!" But, as Peter reminds us, Freddy was just one person out of 23 men from Braughing who died. If it were possible to write books about the lives of every person who was killed, how many libraries would they fill?

This book skilfully illuminates just one man's short life – making the horror of a tragic war alive and touchable. Through Freddy's eyes we can sit in the trenches, march mile upon mile carrying 35lbs of kit on our backs; but above all we can remember what he, and millions of others, suffered with a deeper understanding.

For this we owe Peter – but above all Freddy – a great debt.

Mary Nokes
President, Braughing Local History Society

INTRODUCTION

In the summer of 2012 the quintessentially English village of Braughing, hidden away in rural East Hertfordshire, won Village of the Year for Hertfordshire, a competition organised by the Campaign to Protect Rural England.

If we were to take a journey back in time to one hundred years ago, the architecture of the village then was very similar but there are now in excess of 120 listed buildings, demonstrating the age of many homes. However, there were some significant differences from the Braughing known and loved today.

The Ford in Braughing in 1904

In 1911 the population of Braughing was 949 with an almost even split between the sexes. The area was mainly a farming community, with many small cottages tied to the heavy agricultural work available. There was only a handful of landowners who were the main employers. These cottages were often overcrowded and sanitary conditions were poor. Families were larger and the extended family played an important part in the home. But life was about to change for those families forever.

During the early part of 1914 the government was preparing for war. However, the general public appear to have been mainly ignorant of the facts. Even newspapers scarcely reported what was looming. On 4 August of that year, Britain declared war on Germany. This conflict became known as 'The Great War'. Many thought initially it would be over by Christmas, but instead it lasted for more than four years until 11 November 1918 when Armistice was declared. During this period more than 65 million military personnel across the world were actively involved with the loss of more than 37 million lives. The war affected towns and villages alike. Everybody would have known someone who was killed in action, evidenced by the presence of war memorials and cemeteries in almost every town and village across the country and other parts of the world.

The impact on Braughing was profound as 129 men and boys went off to war aged as young as 16 and as old as 51 years. This was 27% of the male population, which must have had a significant impact on life back home, in terms of the financial and family support that was absent for such a long time. A staggering fact is that almost one in five of those men and boys who went to war were never to see the village and their families again.

Twenty three men and boys were killed in the brutal warfare, causing absolute devastation to their loved ones. Those that did return had often endured physical injuries or gassing and no doubt many suffered from varying degrees of what we now know as post traumatic stress disorder. Misunderstood and misdiagnosed at that time, it was often seen as a sign of cowardice. Braughing families lost fathers, sons, brothers and husbands, causing irreparable damage for generations to come.

The purpose of this book is to remember all of those men and boys who made that terrifying journey and in particular those who made the ultimate sacrifice for our country. This book follows one such brave soldier from Braughing, attempting to bring to life the story of a boy growing up into a young man, only to be struck down in his prime, before he had any real chance of fulfilling his dreams.

Peter Boylan
Chairman, Braughing Local History Society
18 October 2014

THE BRAUGHING DEAD

Of the 129 Braughing men who joined the forces of the King, 23 died, giving their lives to preserve the freedom of their country and the honour of their King. They are listed below, all aged between 17 and 39 years old.

The information below is extracted from the Golden Book of Braughing and from the death certificates of those men who died in England.

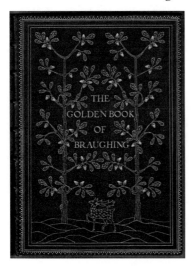

1914

1. Frederick Longman, joined the Royal Fusiliers in 1912 on leaving Cambridge University aged 22, as 2nd Lieutenant; served in France, was promoted to be Lieutenant; was wounded at Vinly, near Chateau Thierry, and was killed at Herlies in N. France on 18th October 1914. He was awarded the 1914 Star.

1915

2. Frederick James Harvey Furneaux, Footman, aged 21, joined the Bedfordshire Regiment as Private and served in France. He was killed in France on 27th April 1915.

3. Thomas Wright, Groom, aged 25, joined the Royal Field Artillery as Private. He was promoted to be Bombardier and died on 6th August 1915 at Hamels Park in Braughing where he had been employed as a groom. The cause of death was tuberculosis. He is buried in Braughing Churchyard.

4. John Dickerson, Gas worker, aged 23, joined the Bedfordshire Regiment as Private; served in France, and was wounded in the eye. He was awarded the 1914 Star and was killed at Loos on 25th September 1915.

5. John Baldwin, Groom, aged 23, joined the 9th Lancers as Private; served at home and died at the Military Hospital in Tidworth in Wiltshire from injuries caused by the accidental fall of a mass of chalk upon him on 28th September 1915. He was then 24 years old.

1916

6. Arthur Cyril Nash, joined the Bedfordshire Regiment as Private, served in France and fell at the Battle of the Somme on 16th September 1916, aged 19.

7. Ramah Deville, Farm Labourer, aged 31, joined the Royal Berkshire Regiment as Private; served in France and was killed on the Somme on 12th November 1916.

8. William Hamilton, Labourer at the watercress beds at Gatesbury in Braughing Parish, aged 37, joined the Gloucestershire Regiment as Private; served in France and was killed near Grandcourt on 18th November 1916.

1917

9. Arthur Smith, Grocer's Manager, aged 29, joined the Royal West Kent Regiment as Private; served in France and Belgium and was killed on 13th March 1917.

10. Frederick Bunce, Labourer, aged 18, joined the Cheshire Regiment as Private and served in France and Belgium. He was killed in action in France on 10th June 1917.

11. Frederick Whyman, Labourer, aged 19, joined the Royal Berkshire Regiment as Private; served in France and was killed on 31st July 1917 aged 21.

12. Charles Lewis, Labourer, aged 19, joined the Hertfordshire Regiment as Private, was

transferred to the Royal Berkshire Regiment. He served in France and Belgium and was killed in action at St Julien on 11th August 1917 on his 21st birthday.

13. William John Skipp, Private in the Northumberland Fusiliers, was killed in action in France on 16th August 1917, aged 39.

14. William Herbert Cook, Horsekeeper, aged 29, joined the West Yorkshire Regiment as Private, served in France. He was reported missing in October 1917 and believed to have fallen in action.

15. Cecil Herbert Shepherd-Cross, Major in the Duke of Lancaster's Own Yeomanry. He died on 15th October 1917 from wounds received near Passchendaele Ridge. He was 39 years old. His name is not recorded on the Braughing War Memorial as it appears on a memorial elsewhere, having been married and moved to London before the war.

16. John William Ball, Bricklayer, aged 28, joined the Somerset Light Infantry as Private; served in France and Belgium, was promoted to be Sergeant and was killed at Passchendaele on 16th December 1917.

1918

17. George Victor Taylor, Labourer, aged 24, joined the Hertfordshire Regiment as Private; served in France and Belgium. He was wounded twice in February 1916 and in September 1917. He died following an operation for a gastric ulcer in Horton War Hospital in Bradford in Yorkshire on 4th January 1918 aged 26. He was awarded the 1914-15 Star.

18. Robert Rogers, Farm Labourer, aged 24, joined the 4th Bedfordshire Regiment as Private; served in France and Belgium and was killed near Ypres on 23rd March 1918.

19. Alderman A Clark, Porter on the Great Eastern Railway, aged 20, joined the Dragoon Guards as Private. He died from wounds in France on 28th March 1918.

Braughing War Memorial 1921

20. Herbert Reginald Parker, Railway Porter, aged 17, joined the Middlesex Regiment as Private; served in France and was killed on 24th April 1918. He was 18 years old.

21. Arthur John Cannon, Engineer Smith, aged 22, joined the Royal Engineers as Sapper and served in Mesopotamia. He was drowned in the Euphrates at Feluja on 9th June 1918.

22. Charles Collins, Gardener, aged 20, joined the Hertfordshire Regiment as Private and served in France and Belgium. He was awarded the 1914 Star, was wounded and was killed in action at Cambrai on 4th September 1918.

1919

23. Ernest Wren, Farm Labourer, aged 18, joined the Machine Gun Corps as Private and served in England and France. He died following complications of influenza in Hertford Hospital on 24th February 1919 aged 20 and is buried in Braughing Churchyard.

EARLY YEARS

Frederick Longman, known by friends and family simply as Freddy, was born on 8 May 1890 at his family's London home, 27 Norfolk Square, close to Paddington station.

Freddy Longman aged 1 year

He was the youngest of four children to Charles James and Harriet Ann Longman. His siblings were Mary aged nine, William aged eight and Sibyl aged five.

Charles James Longman and Harriet Ann Evans in 1880

In 1894 Charles purchased a country estate in Braughing, a rural village in East Hertfordshire. The estate included a large house known as Upp Hall, dating predominantly from the sixteenth century. It lies just outside of the village.

The family spent part of their lives in London, as

Clockwise from top left: Freddy, Sibyl, William and Mary in 1893

Charles was a partner in the famous family publishing business in Paternoster Row.

The family were immediately drawn into the local community, firstly as a key employer; but then in many different ways during the next 40 years. Freddy and his brother and two sisters spent much of their childhood at Upp Hall. The children clearly had a great deal of fun living in the countryside.

As their father was a renowned publisher, many literary friends visited and often stayed with the family at Upp Hall. Amongst their close friends was the author Sir Henry Rider Haggard, most famous for his children's book King Solomon's Mines which was first published by Longmans in 1885. This was a well loved story that was to be read in classrooms for many decades.

Upp Hall and Barn (1934)

Early photograph of Upp Hall entrance (1900)

Rear of Upp Hall and part of the moat (1934)

The Pond at Upp Hall (1934)

Upp Hall from the drive (1934)

Another close friend of the family was prolific children's author, Andrew Lang. Mr Lang was famed for editing a series of coloured fairy tales. The first was the *Blue Fairy Book* published in 1889. Lang was literary adviser to Longmans for many years up until his death in 1912. When Freddy was six years old, Andrew Lang edited *The Animal Story Book* and his father's company published this in 1896. The book was dedicated to Freddy with the following message:

To MASTER FREDERICK LONGMAN

This year our Book for Christmas varies,
Deals not with History nor Fairies
(I can't help thinking, children, you
*Prefer a book which is **not** true).*
We leave these intellectual feasts,
To talk of Fishes, Birds and Beasts.
These – though his aim is hardly steady –
These are, I think, a theme for Freddy!
Trout, though he is not up to fly,
He soon will catch – as well as I!
So, Freddy, take this artless rhyme,
And be a Sportsman in your time!

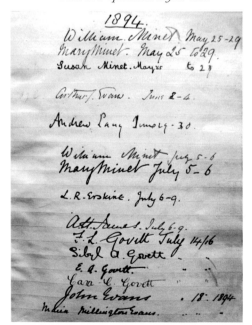

The first entry in the Upp Hall Visitors Book in 1894 including family members and the children's author Andrew Lang

Amateur dramatics became an integral part of the Longman family's Christmas celebrations at Upp Hall.

The Barn at Upp Hall (1934)

A show was produced each year and performed in what was referred to as 'Upp Hall Theatre', which is likely to have been within the walls of the ancient Tithe Barn, just to the west of the house.

Copies of programmes have survived for some shows and include the following:

On 5 January 1898 they performed scenes from *Alice in Wonderland* including 'The Mad Tea Party'.

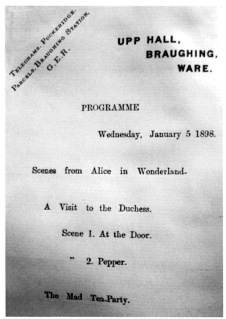

Programme for Alice in Wonderland at Upp Hall (1898)

New Years Eve 1898 saw a production of 'Rumpelstiltzkin' (a children's story by the Brothers Grimm) with Freddy playing the lead role; Mary as King Pompous; William as the Miller; and Sibyl playing Lady Priscilla. This story had been included in Andrew Lang's *The Blue Fairy Book*.

Upp Hall Theatre.

New Years Eve, 1898

Rumpelstiltzkin,

Dramatis Personae.

King Pompous	M Longman.
Miller	W Longman.
Rumpelstiltzkin	F Longman.
Lord Lollipop	N James.
Lady Fenella	N James.
Lady Dulcibella	M James.
Lady Priscilla	S Longman
Miranda	S Minet.
&	
The Royal Heir.	

Upp Hall Theatre programme for New Years Eve production of Rumpelstiltzkin (1898)

On 13 January 1900 the show produced was *Creature of Impulse*. This was a stage play written by W S Gilbert in 1870. It is a story about an unwanted and ill tempered old fairy who enchants people into behaving in a manner opposite to their natures. Freddy acted the part of Boomblehardt, a miser. William played Peter, a young farmer; Mary was 'a strange old lady'; and Sibyl was Pipette, the landlady's niece. The play was set in a public house called 'The Three Pigeons' and included several songs.

At Christmas 1900 the family performed the well known Dickens' story *Nicholas Nickleby* with Sibyl playing Mrs Nickleby and Freddy playing the part of The Keeper. Photographs of this production have survived with Freddy, Sibyl and family friends in costume.

On 2 January 1903 the family performed *Rosencrantz and Guildenstern*, a short comic play by

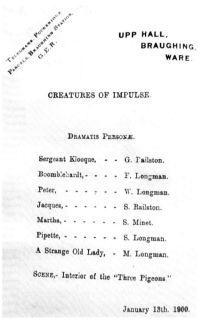

UPP HALL,
BRAUGHING,
WARE.

TELEGRAMS PUCKERIDGE
PARCELS, BRAUGHING STATION.
G.E.R.

CREATURES OF IMPULSE.

DRAMATIS PERSONÆ.

Sergeant Klooque,	G. Railston.
Boomblehardt,	F. Longman.
Peter,	W. Longman.
Jacques,	S. Railston.
Martha,	S. Minet.
Pipette,	S. Longman.
A Strange Old Lady,	M. Longman.

SCENE,- Interior of the "Three Pigeons."

January 13th. 1900.

Programme for Creatures of Impulse at Upp Hall (1900)

W S Gilbert written in 1874, a parody of Shakespeare's *Hamlet*. Mary starred as King Claudius and their cousin Susan Minet who lived at neighbouring Hadham Hall was Queen Gertrude. Meanwhile, William played the part of Hamlet and Sibyl was Ophelia. Freddy played a more minor part as 'First Player'.

Freddy playing the part of the Keeper in Nicholas Nickleby at Upp Hall on 30th December 1901

Dame Joan Evans, Freddy's aunt and half sister to his mother, wrote about her memories of visiting Upp Hall as a child in her autobiography, *Prelude & Fugue* published in 1964. (p 33)

'In the late summer we generally went away to Nannie's home; and sometimes we went to stay afterwards for about a fortnight at my half-sister's house, Upp Hall, on the other side of Hertfordshire; a picturesque, dilapidated Jacobean house of dull and time-stained brick, with the remains of a moat and a row of aspens that rustled like rain. It was a charming place, and though I was afraid of my brother-in-law [Charles], Harriet herself radiated an atmosphere of serenity, and her daughter Sibyl was like her. The door opened into a hall, wide and dark and quiet, that still had its medieval screens. Through this one went into

Harriet's own sitting room, very small and exquisitely fresh and neat, hung with old samplers and needlework pictures, with wide doors opening on to the garden. In the hall one heard the aspens, and here one heard the bees.

The landing held a great cabinet full of dolls' china services and old toys; and upstairs was the family's dolls'-house. It was a delightful place for a child to stay in; for beyond the house itself was a vast barn, with strange echoes and all sorts of things hidden in its depths, such as old croquet sets and archery targets; and the garden itself went on into half wild spinneys and orchards full of the reddest apples I have ever known. There are certain designs by William Morris – "Fruit," for instance – that in their easy repose and antique richness always remind me of Upp Hall.'

Dining Room at Upp Hall

Drawing Room at Upp Hall

Mrs Longman's Bedroom at Upp Hall

Library at Upp Hall

Freddy playing croquet at Upp Hall –
17th September 1910

Freddy and his family were supported by a significant array of staff who worked in the house and on the estate. In 1910, this amounted to no less than ten staff and included roles such as butler, footman, groom, gardener, gamekeeper, coachman, cook, kitchen maid, ladies maid and housemaid.

An important role model in Freddy's life was a housemaid called Louisa Ricket. Known by the family as Loo, she was born in 1862 in Abbots Langley in Hertfordshire close to the childhood home of Mrs Longman. Her father worked as a paper maker presumably employed at the paper mills owned by other members of the Longman family. Shortly after the marriage of Charles and Harriet, Loo joined their

household and remained with them for the rest of her working life. She became a highly trusted confidante of Mrs Longman and took an active interest in the children. The children in return responded to Loo's personality and developed a close bond with her as they grew up. It is noticeable that Loo was the one member of staff Freddy wrote to during the war.

Louisa Ricket, housemaid to the
family taken in 1899

Following the death of Charles Longman in 1934 Loo moved with Mrs Longman and looked after her until Harriet's death in 1938. Loo retired to Carshalton in Surrey. She died on 6 April 1950 at a nursing home in Cheam, Surrey aged 87.

1895 to 1899 – Worie's Class

Freddy's first education was with a private

Male household staff at Upp Hall in 1910. Left to right: Back row: Phillips. Clark, J Roberts, Collins, Adnams, S Carr. Front row: Moor, Holman, A Hemmings, Robinson

Female household staff in 1910. Left to right: Back row: Agnes Windiatt, Ann Ward, Martha Heath (standing), Mrs Kurtz, L Ricket. Front row: Ada Dickinson, Florrie Hobbs, Ellen Warmsbury

governess, known by the family simply as Worie. She taught a small class of young children. There is little known about Worie, but a group photograph has survived of her with the children she taught.

Worie's Class 1897 Left to Right: Dick Worsley, Marjory Bryce, Freddy Longman, Margey Haxley, Cecil Farrer, Worie, Sybil Balfour, Nigel Bryce, Roland Bryce, Sybil Longman, Dorothy Wright

1899 to 1903 – Preparatory School, Eastbourne

He was then sent to a preparatory boarding school known as Mr Wilkinson's school in Warren Hill, Eastbourne.

Warren Hill School, Eastbourne

Little is known of his time there. When at home Freddy became a member of the Braughing Rifle Club, which had been introduced into the village by his father, an extremely keen rifleman. A range was built and maintained at Chalk Lodge, then belonging to the Longman estate. The shooting season started with an annual general meeting of the rifle club in April each year and ended with a prize day in September. The parish magazine reveals that on 5 September 1903 Freddy won first prize in a boy's competition at the age of 13 years.

Freddy whilst at school in Eastbourne in 1903

1903 to 1907 – Harrow School

In the autumn of 1903 Freddy moved to Harrow School in north-west London. He boarded in Mr Graham's house, which in 1912 became known as Rendall's House, its current name.

He was a keen sportsman and excelled in football, swimming and boxing. The school magazine, known as *The Harrovian*, records some of Freddy's sporting achievements.

Freddy with his father in the garden at Upp Hall on 15th July 1905

Soon after arriving, in November 1903 he joined the school Rifle Corps to further pursue a skill in which he clearly already excelled. By May 1907 Freddy is described as a Corporal. He was a member of the school team at this time. Then in October 1907 he was promoted to Sergeant.

On 7 March 1907 Freddy won a boxing competition when he managed to dodge his opponent's swinging blows and became the school's champion feather weight boxer.

In June 1907 Freddy won the three-legged race with a fellow student in the House Sports day.

Freddy also joined the elite group of scholars at Harrow that were known as Dolphins, a group of accomplished swimmers. To become a Dolphin boys had to complete a five length course of Ducker Pool, a private outdoor swimming pool in Harrow, at the time the largest in the country. They had to demonstrate a range of different strokes, overcome obstacles, climb out and dive in, all to be completed within 19 minutes. Being a Dolphin provided the added benefit of being allowed to wear trunks, other boys had to swim naked.

In July that year Freddy won first place in a swimming competition in Ducker pond, when he retrieved 11 china eggs. However, as he had won this competition in 1905, he had to forfeit the prize to somebody else.

Ducker Pond at Harrow School (1905)

Harrow football is an unusual game with its own set of rules. It is played on a hill with a doughnut shaped ball to prevent it rolling away. Freddy began playing and on 15 December 1905 he was a member of Mr Graham's XI in the Cock House Match. His team won.

Freddy in his football kit at Harrow School

In December 1906 Freddy is again listed as a member of Mr Graham's team, who won the match against Mr Owen's. As a result of this they went through to the semi final against Mr Davidson's on 8 December. His team won again and Freddy was presented with a fez, a type of striped cap worn by the school's football XI.

In November 1907 Freddy represented the school at football. The school won 6-0. At the end of the year *The Harrovian* published a summary report for each of the school's Football XI members. Freddy is described as playing top wing position. 'A clever hard working player both in attack and defence; rather light but scrums well, when not on all fours; or shot.'

Freddy left Harrow at the end of 1907 but was to maintain a close link with the school for the rest of his life. In particular, he was well known for the work he did at school and afterwards with the Harrow Road Mission helping children less fortunate than himself.

It was whilst he was at Harrow, that Freddy produced a series of fine wild life drawings including insects, mice, birds and hedgehogs.

Insects drawn from specimens by Freddy Longman

Field Mouse by Freddy Longman (1905)

Blackbird by Freddy Longman (1905)

Hedgehog by Freddy Longman (1907)

Field Mouse by Freddy Longman (1907)

He also set about writing poetry and wrote about himself as part of a series he called *The Upp Ballads*, complete with cartoon drawings.

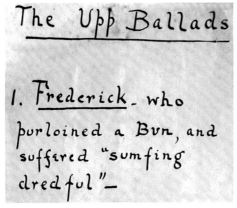

The Upp Ballads by Freddy Longman

Frederick – who purloined a Bun, and suffered "sumfing dredful" –

> Here is cruel Frederick see!
> A horrid wicked boy was he;
> He bawled at 'terriers', khaki-clad,
> Until he drove them almost mad.
> He taught his dog to bark and bite
> Whene'er the Vicar came in sight;
> And oh! Far worse than all beside,
> He teased his Louie till she cried.

> But wusser still is yet to come –
> He ate a little slum child's bun!

The children numbered 9 times 4,
> The buns were 36 – no more;
> The 35 were duly doled
> When Frederick's Mamma was told
> (And thro' the house the dire news flew)
> 'Alas! There was a bun too few!
> Who <u>could</u> have played the sorry trick?
> Why none but cruel Frederick!

> So Frederick had to go to rest;
> The bun lay heavy on his chest!
> The doctor came at Ma's request,
> And made a very great to-do,
> And gave him nasty physic too.

> But the little waif is back in Town,
> Her nose and cheeks a lovely brown;
> She seats herself in Daddy's chair,
> And laughs to see the nice things there:
> But nobly keeps from everyone
> The tale of Frederick and the Bun –

In September 1907, at the age of 17, Freddy, the youngest member of the Braughing Rifle Club, won second prize in a shooting competition held at the range at Chalk Lodge. The following September his father presented Freddy with the Donegal Badge for shooting, awarded by the National Rifle Association. In 1909 Freddy was elected to join the club committee. That summer he began to coach local lads to shoot, which resulted in a contest with boys from Buntingford and High Cross in the September. Of course, the Braughing boys won, thanks to their new coach.

19

Freddy's dog Bob taken in 1914

Jock, one of family dogs outside the front door of Upp Hall circa 1912

Freddy nursing his dog Dan at Upp Hall in 1905

Freddy was always surrounded by dogs at home as a child. These pets were invariably terrier type dogs and spaniels with names such as Dan, Jock, Jet and Bob.

1909 to 1912 – Pembroke College, Cambridge

According to his application form for admission, dated 9 December 1907, Freddy stated that he wished to read medicine.

He went up to Cambridge University as a member of Pembroke College on 21 October 1909. He achieved a 2nd class pass in Part 1 Chemistry in the Michaelmas Term of 1910; and a 3rd class pass in part 2 Chemistry in the Easter Term of 1911.

He gained a 2nd class pass in part 1 Military subjects in the Michaelmas Term of 1911 and a 2nd class pass in Part 2 of the special examination in Military subjects in Easter Term, 1912.

He graduated on 15 June 1912 with an Ordinary Bachelor of Arts degree in Chemistry and in Military subjects, the latter very much in vogue before the First World War. Only two months later, he was transferred into the Royal Fusiliers as an officer.

Pembroke Ball in 1911, including Freddy in the middle of the group with his mother Harriet.

Pembroke College, Cambridge taken in 1911

Freddy Longman aged 22, taken whilst a student at Cambridge in 1912

Pembroke Ball in 1912, including Freddy in the centre of the group. His mother is also featured in the row in front of him.

Freddy outside Upp Hall in 1909

May Week, Cambridge. Freddy in a punt alongside Kitty Rayner with his mother in front with Mary Minet from Hadham Hall.

May Week at Pembroke College, Cambridge. Left to right: Back row: Mr Pilditch, Lilias Haggard, Sybil Longman, Charles Longman, Miss Bates, Miss Gabain, Miss Courtes. Front row: Freddy Longman, Miss Pilditch, Mrs Pilditch, Mr Courtes, Harriet Longman, Mr PH Pilditch, Miss Gabain

A MILITARY CAREER

Although Freddy was well known in Braughing for his skills with a gun, both at the rifle range and also when out shooting with the family, he first became interested in a military career whilst studying at Pembroke College, Cambridge. The universities were important recruitment grounds for future officers and Freddy was clearly attracted to the life of an army officer. He became a Private in the Cambridge University Officers Training Corps. On 21 August 1910, whilst he was still an undergraduate, he applied for and was granted a commission with the 1st Battalion of the Hertfordshire Regiment, as announced in *The London Gazette* on 18 October 1910.

1st Battalion, The Hertfordshire Regiment; Cadet Private Frederick Longman, from the Cambridge University Contingent, Senior Division, Officers Training Corps, to be Second Lieutenant. (To be supernumerary.) Dated 19th October, 1910.

London Gazette October 1910

He was restored to the establishment as reported in *The London Gazette* on 20 December 1910. This meant he was longer supernumerary.

1st Battalion, The Hertfordshire Regiment; Supernumerary Second Lieutenant Frederick Longman is restored to the establishment. Dated 24th November, 1910.

London Gazette December 1910

Almost two years later Freddy was transferred to the Royal Fusiliers. *The London Gazette* on 6 August 1912 recorded -

INFANTRY.
The Royal Fusiliers (City of London Regiment), Dated 13th February, 1912, but not to carry pay or allowances prior to 7th August, 1912:—
    Second Lieutenant Frederick Longman, from 1st Battalion The Hertfordshire Regiment.
    Second Lieutenant Maurice Edward Coxhead, from Unattached List Territorial Force.

London Gazette August 1912

Shortly after transferring to the Royal Fusiliers, Freddy very proudly paraded around the gardens at Upp Hall in his ceremonial dress uniform including a bearskin with his family looking on.

Above and top left on page 23: Second Lieutenant Frederick Longman sporting his new ceremonial uniform including bearskin following transfer from Hertfordshire Regiment to the Royal Fusiliers in 1912.

Freddy continued to participate in sports as he had in school and university. He particularly excelled in boxing and swimming.

4th Battalion Royal Fusiliers – winners of shield for Aquatic Sports in 1913. Freddy in shorts and jacket

In August 1914 Freddy was promoted to Lieutenant as reported in *The London Gazette* on 9 October 1914.

INFANTRY.

The Royal Fusiliers (City of London) Regiment, The undermentioned Second Lieutenants to be Lieutenants:—

Frederick Longman. Dated 24th August, 1914.

Maurice E. Coxhead. Dated 5th September, 1914.

London Gazette October 1914

Freddy in his new Royal Fusiliers dress uniform in 1912 at Upp Hall. Left to right: Bob, Sibyl Longman, Harriet Longman, Freddy Longman, Jane Evans, Kitty Rayner and Geoffrey Rayner

REGIMENTAL WAR DIARY

The following transcript forms part of the War Diaries maintained by each regiment throughout the war to record activity of each operational unit. This diary recounts the daily activity of the 4th Battalion of the Royal Fusiliers who had joined the 9th Brigade of the 3rd Division in France. This information in this chapter is a transcription of that diary between August and October 1914 and helps to build the evidence available about the lives of Freddy and his comrades during this period.

Second Lieutenant Frederick Longman of 4th Battalion Royal Fusiliers 1914

August 1914

Hour, Place, Date	Summary of Events and Information
Parkhurst 6.10 pm 4th Aug 1914	Mobilization ordered. 2 Companies Fortress Manning.
Parkhurst 5th Aug 1914	1st day of mobilization. 2 officers and 3 N.C.Os proceeded to Hounslow on Conducting duty. Two Companies Fortress Manning.
Parkhurst 6th Aug 1914 5.15 a.m. 11 pm 9.25am	2nd day of mobilization. 384 reservists joined from Hounslow 2 Companies returned to Barracks from Fortress Manning. All horses bought, establishment complete. 1 officer and 3 N.C.Os proceeded for conducting duty to Depot.
Parkhurst 7th Aug 1914 2 a.m.	3rd day of mobilization. About 340 Reservists arrived from Depot.
Parkhurst 8th Aug 1914 7 pm.	Sent 1 Captain, 2 Subalterns & 15 N.C.Os to Depot for new units. About 40 N.C.Os & men joined from Depot. Alterations had to be made to Sa a Carts. Reported mobilized 11.50 pm.
Parkhurst 9th Aug 1914	5th day of mobilization. Transport inspected by C.O. Reservists drilled by Companies.
Parkhurst 10th Aug 1914 3.20pm	Reservists fired Range Practices at NEWTOWN. Details left for FALMOUTH strength 3 officers & 234 other ranks. 6th day of mobilization. Establishment of officers reduced.
Parkhurst 11th Aug 1914 10 a.m.	7th day of mobilization. Battalion Drill followed by route march about 9 miles, very hot, many casualties amongst Reservists. Sergeant tailor left for Depot.
Parkhurst 12th Aug 1914 7 p.m. 7 p.m.	8th day of mobilization. 13 reservists joined from Depot. Orders received to embark at Cowes on 13th Aug.
9 a.m. Parkhurst 13th Aug 5 p.m. Southampton 6 p.m. "	Left Parkhurst for Southampton Embarked on MARTABAN Sailed for Havre
4 a.m. HAVRE 14th Aug 8.20 a.m. " " " 1 p.m. Rest Camp " "	Arrived at HAVRE Left HAVRE for Rest Camp, about 7 miles away. Arrived at Rest Camp. Many men fell out on the march owing to the great heat & the large number of reservists in the Battalion. No extra transport was available for extra rations therefore our transport was overloaded.
Rest Camp 15th Aug	Remained in Rest Camp. Very wet weather.
11.15 am HAVRE 16th Aug 12 noon " " " 3.30 pm " " "	Entrained for Concentration area at 11.15 a.m. Entrainment completed. Train started.
6.50 a.m. BUSIGNY 17th Aug 7.30 a.m. LANDRECIES " 9.30 a.m. LANDRECIES 11.30am NOYELLES	Train arrived. Train arrived. Left LANDRECIES & marched to NOYELLES about 7 miles. Arrived and were billeted there. 23 men fell out.
NOYELLES 18th Aug 11am	Billetted. Battalion Route march about 3 miles. 20 men fell out. Fine weather.

Hour, Place, Date	Summary of Events and Information
NOYELLES 19th Aug	Billetted. Brigade Route march about 8 miles, one man fell out.
10 am NOYELLES 20th Aug 2.15 pm TAISNAIRES	Moved to new billets at TAISNAIRES about 2 miles away. Brigade Route march about 6 miles, 4 men fell out. 18 men sent sick to LANDRECIES.
5 am TAISNAIRES 21st Aug 10 am LA LONGUEVILLE	Started as Advance Guard. Arrived after a march of about 10 miles, fine day. Billetted.
5.30 am LA LONGUEVILLE 22nd Aug. 6 pm NIMY just north of MONS	Started. Crossed Belgian Frontier near MALPLAQUET. Advance guard. Took up an outpost position guarding crossing over the Canal. Had orders to hold on to this position as long as possible. Quiet night.
MONS 23rd Aug.	Still holding outpost position. A certain amount of desultory firing took place in the early morning. We wounded & captured two Uhlan officers.
About 11 am	The Germans started to attack us seriously with apparently at least four battalions of infantry, also Cavalry and Artillery. We suffered severely on the bridge over the Canal by rifle and Artillery fire. The machine guns had a particularly trying time. Practically all the detachment including Lieut. M[aurice] Dease, the Machine Gun officer were killed or wounded. Lieut Dease and Pte Godley both displayed the most conspicuous gallantry in working the guns after they had been wounded. The guns having finally been disabled by Artillery fire had to be abandoned.
1.10 pm. MONS 23rd Aug. 1.40 " " " "	First order to retire was given. Final order to retire was given.
About 3.30pm " " "	Successful retirement through MONS accomplished. The battalion carried out this most difficult manoeuvre with the greatest steadiness. The total Casualties sustained by the battalion at MONS were about 112 killed & wounded including 7 officers. Most of these Casualties had unfortunately to be left behind.
About 7 pm CIPLEY 23rd Aug	Arrived CIPLEY and bivouacked there until about 2 a.m. 24th Aug.

Hour, Place, Date	Summary of Events and Information
2 am. CIPLEY 24th Aug	Attached to 7th Inf. Bde & marched to take up a position just north of CIPLEY in conjunction with 7th Inf. Bde.
10 am. GENLY 24th Aug.	At dawn on 24th Aug the Germans attacked; not very heavily but we had orders to retire & did so through GENLY about 10 a.m.
10.30pm BERMERIES	Marched to BERMERIES, arrived about 10.30 pm having marched about 20 miles. Bivouacked.
5 am BERMERIES 25th Aug.	Moved from BERMERIES in the direction of POTELLE. A great deal of fighting took place between aeroplanes. Our planes apparently put a German Zeppelin out of action.
About 10am 25th Aug.	Our battalion brought down a German aeroplane by rifle fire.
About 6.15 pm 25th Aug.	Arrived at INCHY. Billetted. 2 Coys on outpost.
About 6 am. 26th Aug	Retired on a position which had already been entrenched S.E. of INCHY.
About 9 am 26th INCHY position	Suffered slightly from shrapnell fire bursting very accurately into a sunken road in which we took cover as reserve battalion. 2nd Lt Sampson was wounded & removed to Field Ambulance. We suffered few other Casualties as the Germans did not attack heavily at this point of the line.
2.30pm INCHY position 26th Aug.	Received order to retire & did so in a S. westerly direction to HARGINCOURT.
10 am. HARGINCOURT 27th Aug.	Arrived having marched all night
6.30 pm. VERMAND	Arrived & bivouacked having been under arms continuously since Saturday 22nd Aug.
1 a.m. 28th Aug. VERMAND	Started & marched continuously through HAM till 6.30 pm. when we arrived at CRISOLLES & billetted.
CRISOLLES 29th Aug 1 pm " " "	Billetted. Ordered out to hold a position covering CRISOLLES. Killed two Uhlans about 5 pm. About 7 pm received orders to retire. Retired in a Southerly direction & marched all night through NOYON.
About 10am MONTOIS 30th	Halted for some hours. Resumed march and arrived at MONTOIS about 6 pm. Billetted for night of 30th – 31st.
31st Aug 7am	Left MONTOIS, marched in a Southerly direction, very hot. Arrived at VAUCIENNES about 5 pm, billetted.

September 1914

Hour, Place, Date	Summary of Events and Information
6.30 am Sept 1st 8pm	Left VAUCIENNES. Rear guard. Arrived BOUILLANCY after a long & very hot march, billeted in "battle billets."
4.30 am Sept 2nd	Left BOUILLANCY & marched to PENCHARD arriving about 2 pm. Billeted, quiet night.
7 am. Sept 3rd	Left PENCHARD, marched through MEAUX, arrived at LE MANS FARM about 4.30 p.m, billeted.
1.30 pm. Sept 4th LE MANS FARM	Ordered to leave & to take up a defensive position south of LA HAUTE MAISON. Ordered to retire from here at 10.30 pm. Did so.
Sept 5th CHATRES	Marched all night arriving at CHATRES at 7 am after long & trying march. 1 officer & 90 1st reinforcements joined.
6.30 am. Sept 6th CHATRES	<u>Advance resumed.</u> Advance guard. Advanced in Northerly direction. About 10 a.m. halted for some hours. Received orders to advance by LUMIGNY & were informed that enemy was retreating. Arrived LUMIGNY about 8 pm. billeted.
12 noon Sept 7th LUMIGNY	Left LUMIGNY. Last Bn. in Division. Crowded, uncomfortable march owing to not being clear of 2nd Div. Arrived at LA MARTROY about 7 pm, billeted. 2nd reinforcements of 1 officer & 93 men joined.
6 a.m. LA MARTROY 8 Sept.	Advanced in a Northerly direction. Held up for some hours. by evening at ORLY. Finally dislodged them and continued advance. Arrived at LES FAUCHERES about 8 p.m billeted.
5 a.m. LES FAUCHERES 9th Sept	Resumed advance crossed R. [River] MARNE unopposed. Met enemy on north side of river. A good deal of fighting took place. Battalion not engaged. Bivouacked at LA LONGUE FERME. 2 Coys slept in trenches.
5 a.m. Sept 10th	Left LA LONGUE FERME, advanced northwards in pursuit of enemy. Bn. Advance Guard. Got in touch with enemy near VEUILLY. Shelled his transport & drove him from his position North of VEUILLY, in cooperation with 1st Corps on our right. Killed & wounded large numbers of enemy who finally surrendered. We had a few casualties including 2 officers seriously and 2 officers slightly wounded. Arrived DAMMARD about 4.30 p.m. billeted. [Frederick Longman wounded].
7.30 am. DAMMARD Sept 11th	Left and marched to GRAND ROZOY. Arrived about 1.30 pm. billeted. No firing heard for first time for many days.
6 a.m. GRAND ROZOY Sept 12th	Left & marched in N. Easterly direction. In touch with enemy on LA VESLE R. [River] at BRAINE. Slight opposition. Our Cavalry had skirmish with enemy on northern bank of river, captured enemy position. Billeted at BRENELLE Very wet afternoon & night.
8 a.m. BRENELLE 13th Sept. 11 p.m. VAILLY	Left billets & marched in a N.W. direction towards VAILLY. A great deal of artillery firing took place all round. The Battalion halted under cover & took no active part. At dusk resumed march on VAILLY & at about 11 p.m. crossed R. AISNE by improvised bridge. Crossing completed about 11.30 p.m. then ordered to take up a position covering VAILLY on the heights, North of the village.

Hour, Place, Date	Summary of Events and Information
Sept 14th	Arrived at position near LA ROUGE MAISON FARM just after midnight. No attack during the night. At dawn which was foggy & very wet the Germans attacked with strong Artillery and Machine Gun Support. The battalion held its ground for some time but owing to the Regiment on its right giving away had to retire to a sunken road about 200 yards south of LA ROUGE MAISON. This position we held onto. We had many casualties including 5 officers Killed wounded & missing & about 200 other ranks also killed wounded or missing.
Night of 14th – 15th Sept.	The enemy made a night attack but were repulsed with rifle fire & bayonet.
Sept 15th	Holding on to position in sunken road, which we have strongly entrenched & traversed. Enemy shelled us a good deal but we only had two casualties.
Night of 15th – 16th	Very wet night. Night attack by enemy not serious. Was repulsed by rifle fire.
Sept 16th	Still holding on to position. All ranks doing splendidly. Still improving our entrenchments. The enemy can be seen at about 2 to 300 yards from our position, also entrenched. A good deal of sniping taken place but we have very few casualties.
Sept 17th	Still holding on to position. Very wet day everyone wet through as we have no cover. The enemy have been shelling the valley south of us & the bridge at VAILLY ever since we came here, but have not done much damage.
Night of 17th – 18th	Expected night attack from rumours of inhabitants. Stood to arms all night, no attack.
Sept 18th	Still holding on to position. Fine day. Quiet but very wet night, everyone wet through.
Sept 19th	Fine day. Got very severe shelling from enemy commencing about 2.30 p.m. Our own guns hardly replying at all owing to the long range. We had several casualties. Heavy shelling by enemy's artillery at short range continued till about 6 p.m. when it stopped & there was a general advance of the enemy's infantry. They attacked heavily but were repulsed with many casualties by rifle fire. Some of the enemy appeared to get lost in the darkness & there was some confusion amongst them. One prisoner of the 64th Regt. was captured.
Night of 19th – 20th	Quiet & fine night.

Hour, Place, Date	Summary of Events and Information
20th Sept.	Enemy resumed the attack at dawn but did not press it home. Attack died away after about 2 hours. Enemy still continued to shell us accurately, & we had a few casualties. Our guns gave us much more support today than they had done before.
5 pm	Relieved by the Lincolnshire Regt. after having been 7 days in the firing line. Joined by 3rd reinforcements, 1 officer & 92 other ranks. [*Including Frederick Longman*]
Night of 20th – 21st Sept	About 3 am, 21st 2 Regts of 6th Div moved to MAISON ROUGE position & we retired across the AISNE to COURCELLES & billeted there for a much needed rest.
21st Sept.	Colonel McMahon was complemented by Gen. Hamilton, Com.r [Commander] of 3rd Div. [*General Hubert Hamilton, killed on 14th October*] and by Gen. [Frederick] Shaw, Comr. of 9th Inf. [Infantry] Bde on the work done by the battalion during the past week. About 4 pm. Sir John French visited the Battalion and expressed to men and officers the appreciation of their work during the last week. [*Sir John French was the Commander in Chief of the British Expeditionary Force*].
22nd Sept. COURCELLES	Billeted. Joined by the whole Brigade, which now became temporarily Reserve to the Army. Joined by 4th reinforcements, 2 officers & 156 other ranks.
23rd Sept. "	Billeted. Resting.
24th Sept. "	Billeted. Resting.
5pm COURCELLES 25th Sept.	Left COURCELLES with Lincolnshire Regt. to march through VAILLY to take up a position north of this village, held by 8th Inf. Bde.
VAILLY 9 p.m. " "	Arrived at position on high ground just out side & N.W. of VAILLY & west of our original position at ROUGE MAISON. About 10 pm. took over position from Royal Irish Regt. Lincolnshire Regt. in position on our left Middlesex on our right. The position is a curious one; very wooded in places with trenches facing in all directions. It is commanded by the enemy & we get severely shelled. It is a difficult position to hold by day as there is no field of fire. It is a fairly strong position at night as the ground is very difficult for the enemy to attack over. He would probably have to come by the roads which we have strongly barricaded.
VAILLY 26th Sept.	In position. Shelled by enemy, No casualties. Joined by remainder of 9th Bde. Northumberland Fusiliers now on our right instead of the Middlesex Regt.
27th Sept.	In position. Shelled mildly by enemy, No casualties. Fine weather.
28th Sept.	In position & improving it. Making a second line of defence round Village by loop holing walls etc. Still being shelled by enemy. A few casualties amongst Lincolnshire Regt.
Night of 28th – 29th	About 10 pm. a good deal of rifle fire heard on our right in the direction of ROUGE MAISON. Stood to Arms for about 1 hour. No attack on our position.
29th	In position. Nothing of importance happened. Fine day. Nights getting very cold.
30th	In position. Nothing of importance happened.

October 1914

Hour, Place, Date	Summary of Events and Information
Oct 1st in position VAILLY	Very fine day nothing of importance happened. 5th Fusiliers & Scots Fusiliers left for unknown destination.
Oct 2nd " " " 7.30 p.m. " " "	No enemy fire today. Most of them seem to have gone. 9th Bde relieved by Shropshire & Buffs. Marched for unknown destination in Southerly direction. Marched all night through BRAINE. Arrived at farm just north of SERVENAY at about 4 a.m. (Oct 3rd) billeted for day.
Oct 3rd	Left farm near SERVENAY at 5.45 pm. marched on TROESNES. Arrived at about 12.30 a.m. Oct 4th beautiful moonlight night. Billeted.
Oct 4th	Billeted at TROESNES. Left about 6 pm. Marched in Westerly direction, through FOREST of RETZ to CREPY-EN-VALOIS, arrived about 2 am. Oct 5th. Long march, fine night. Very severe night marching the last three nights, average about 18 miles.
Oct 5th	Billeted at CREPY. Left at 6 pm, marched to ROBERVAL, arrived at 12 midnight, billeted.
Oct 6th	Left ROBERVAL at 6.45 a.m. marched to LONGUEIL PONT, crossing R. OISE by pontoon bridge of barges, entrained there 1 p.m. for unknown destination. Arrived at AILLY SUR SOMME about 7 p.m. Remained there all night in train (night of 6th – 7th)
Oct 7th	Detrained at PONT REMY about 12 noon. Marched to BUIGNY ST MACLOU. Arrived about 5 p.m. Billeted with remainder of Bde.
Oct 8th	Billeted at BUIGNY
Oct 9th	Left BUIGNY at 1.45 a.m. & marched to TOLLEN. Arrived about 7 a.m billeted for day.
Oct 10th	Left TOLLEN about 1.a.m: marched to HESDIN & from there were taken in French Motor Lorries to SAINS total distance about 25 miles. Billeted at SAINS, joined by 9 officers.
Oct 11th	Left SAINS about 7.30 a.m. marched to point south of Canal at RONCQ billeted.
Oct 12th	Left billets at 7 a.m and marched towards VIELLE CHAPELLE. Arrived there about 3 pm. A certain amount of shelling done by the enemy. 8th Bde attacked and did not make much progress. 9th Bde in reserve. About 5 p.m. retired to billets at LE CORNET MALO.
Oct 13th	Left billets at about 4 a.m. marched to VIELLE CHAPELLE. Arrived there about 5 a.m. Bn in Divisional Reserve. Remained all day. A great deal of firing & fighting took place along the line BOUT DE VILLE – LA COUTURE. 7th 8th & part of 9th Bde engaged. Also Artillery. Country very flat & close intercepted by dykes no field of fire or view.
Oct 14th . .	Remained all day billeted as Divl Reserve. A good deal of firing Eastwards. No news can be obtained. Joined by 5th reinforcements 2 officers & 174 O.R. [other ranks]. Gen Hamilton (Comr 3rd Div) killed by stray shrapnel. At about 7 pm. heavy firing heard to East. Stood to arms for about 2 hours, firing died away.

Hour, Place, Date	Summary of Events and Information
Oct 15th	Still in same billets. Gen. Colin Mackenzie took over command of 3rd Div. [*he only lasted two weeks. He was relieved of his command following the inconclusive result at the Battle of La Bassée*] Moved with 5th Fusiliers at 1 p.m. on BOUT DE VILLE with orders to cooperate with 8th Bde on right & advance & take main road running South E. from ESTAIRES. Deployed from BOUT DE VILLE & meeting with little opposition occupied this road by about 5 p.m. Entrenched East of road night of 15th 16th. All quiet very foggy morning, in touch with the French on our left.
Oct 16th	Continued advance on line of RUE DU BOIS which was reached in the afternoon very little opposition; reached a line east of AUBERS astride RUE D'ENFER at about 5 p.m. dug ourselves in, battle outposts, night of 16th 17th. A few casualties from snipers. Quiet night.
Oct 17th	Resumed advance at 7 a.m. & occupied AUBERS without opposition about 10 a.m. Continued advance on HERLIES met with opposition from rifle fire. Occupied HERLIES at dusk. About 10 casualties including 1 officer killed. Battle outposts night of 17th 18th.
Oct 18th	Occupying HERLIES. Shelled a good deal by Germans we are holding loop holed houses & trenches on outskirts of village. 5th Fusiliers are in support in village. About 5 pm Scots Fusiliers on our right attacked, also 18th Royal Irish on our left. Our artillery gave no support & attack was not successful. French attacked at same time on our left & gained some ground. Their artillery is wonderful & gives their infantry tremendous support. During the attack we held HERLIES & had about 40 casualties. **[Frederick Longman killed]**
19th Oct.	Still in HERLIES. Good deal of shelling all day some casualties. Some firing at night. In the evening the 18th Royal Irish made a very fine attack on PILLY & took it but suffered very severely.
20th Oct.	Very heavily shelled all day. Enemy attacked under this support but made very little impression. Many casualties, including 3 officers. The village of HERLIES was smashed to pieces by heavy shells. Night of 20th 21st retired part of Bn. to farm just west of HERLIES.
21st Oct.	Village more heavily shelled than ever most of houses broken down. No serious attack by infantry, many casualties. Night of 21st 22nd Very heavy night attack on our right held by 5th Div. Shelling & rifle fire most of the night. No serious attack on us. Retired whole line to position ½ mile E. of AUBERS running through LE PLOUICH & LIGNY LE GD [GRAND], entrenched.
Oct 22nd Night of 22nd – 23rd Oct	In trenches under moderate shell fire no casualties. Received orders to withdraw to a prepared position about 4 miles West of AUBERS started 12 midnight.
23 Oct. Night of 23rd 24th Oct	Defensive position taken up. In our section by 2 Bns. Our Bn. in reserve. At PONT DU HEM billeted. Heavy firing about 1 a.m. stood to Arms, no developments.

Hour, Place, Date	Summary of Events and Information
24 Oct.	All Coys in billets but will cover trenches dug in case of shell fire. Ordered out at night to retake trenches evacuated by another Regt. of 8th Bde. But found on arrival at position that this had already been done by Middlesex Regt. Spent all night on the move, but did nothing. Left 1 Coy out as support to 8th Bde. This Coy reformed in billets.
25th	Ordered out about 12 noon to retake trenches evacuated by a Rgt. of 7th Bde. did so, but with several casualties, including 3 officers, 2 killed. Remained in recaptured trenches night of 25th 26th Very wet.
26th Oct.	2 Coys returned to billets at dawn on 26th 2 Coys in billets. 2 Coys in firing line with 7th Bde. Ordered out with 2 Coys about 2 p.m. to support Coys in firing line West of NEUVE CHAPELLE. Found them heavily engaged; the enemy having occupied some of our trenches. Made a night attack to try & recapture them but failed & had very heavy casualties including 8 officers.
27th	Attacked enemy again in cooperation with remains of 6 battalions. Very severe fighting nearly recaptured trenches but were driven back in the end to a new line of trenches. Heavy casualties including 2 officers. Held on to new trenches for night of 27th 28th.
Oct 28th	Only about 8 officers and 350 other ranks left now. Joined by Lts. Stapleton, Brotherton and Routley. Quiet day, some shelling and sniping.
29th Night 29th 30th	Still in same trenches. Relieved about 1 a.m. by Gourkas. Marched to VIELLE CHAPPELLE. Rested for a few hours. Attached to 7th Bde & marched to DOULIEU billeted. Joined by 6th reinforcements about 70 N.C.Os & men.
31st Oct	Left DOULIEU 9 a m, marched to MERRIS billeted.

Acknowledgement

The digitized pages of this regimental war diary are published by the National Archives (Reference: WO/95/1431). Contains public sector information licensed under the Open Government Licence v2.0.

The Officers of 4th Battalion The Royal Fusiliers at Parkhurst 11 August 1914. Top row: Lt Orred Lt Dease 2Lt Longman 2Lt Mead 2Lt Russell 2Lt Hobbs 2Lt Mostyn. Centre row: 2Lt Hardman 2Lt Sampson Lt Steele Capt Packe Capt H Forster Lt Smith Capt F Forster Lt Harding Lt Beazley Lt Tower Capt Byng Lt Cooper Capt Ashburner DSO. Front row: 2Lt Barton Capt Whinney Capt Cole Lt & QM Cross Maj Mallock DSO Lt Col McMahon DSO Lt & Adjt T O'Donnell Capt Le M Carry Capt Bowden-Smith Capt Attwood. Of these 31 officers, 10 would be killed in action before the end of 1914, and at least another three by the end of the War
© Commonwealth War Graves Commission

FREDDY'S JOURNAL

During this period of history it was very common to keep a diary, recording important life changing events as well as the day to day mundane aspects of our existence. Freddy was no exception. He began writing in a new notebook when it became evident that war was inevitable. He continued to write a personal account of his own experiences, the challenges brought about by war and his fears of what lay ahead. At the front of his diary was a photograph of Bob, his terrier dog back home in Braughing, a friend he was clearly very fond of. He does not manage to write every day, but when he can he recounts what has happened since his last entry.

Freddy's dog taken in 1914. This photograph of Bob was attached to the front of Freddy's diary he wrote in France.

The first pages are written in pencil, then in pen and the last pages in pencil. Some of the early pages were written over with a few changes to the original text. Place names are recorded as they are now spelt, but other grammar and spellings are as Freddy wrote them. He posted a section of his journal home on at least one occasion for safe keeping but continued to write until only four days before his death. His personal belongings, including this diary, were returned to his family following his death and have been treasured ever since. Short extracts were published in 1922 in *The Royal Fusiliers in the Great War* by H.C O'Neill. However, this is the first time it has been published in its entirety.

1914

I am starting to write this journal with no great hopes of keeping it up long. But as far as one can see we are at the beginning of a war which will involve nearly all the Nations of Europe, and which will dwarf Napoleon's campaigns and if from time to time I can find the time, or inclination to jot down the impressions of a very junior officer, and any experiences or adventures which may come our way, they may be of interest at any rate to my friends and relations and certainly – if all goes well – to my grand children. So here goes.

Wednesday July 26th [July 29th]

On returning from Freshwater at about 7 pm, where I had been batheing with O'Donel we were greeted with the news that the Precautionary period had been ordered, and we were to man the forts immediately. I went off at about 8.30 with 32 N.C.Os [non-commissioned officers] & men to Yaverland Battery, and by 11 we had taken over the fort & posted all Sentries, guards etc.

Yaverland is a small fort with 3 6" guns and 2 machine guns. Absolutely no precautions had been taken for protection, and trees were growing right up to the walls of the fort, blocking up the loop holes and preventing all field of fire.

During the week we were there I had to put all the men hard at work clearing trees, hedges, putting up wire entanglements, digging trenches, and in fact doing 101 jobs which ought to have been done during the last 20 years.

There were three garrison gunner officers in the fort at a time, but they were constantly changing. All quite pleasant but not exciting. Messing quite good.

Our routine was as follows:

3 a.m.	I went to bed
4 a.m.	Sentries relieved
6.30 a.m.	Breakfasts
7 a.m.	I got up
8 a.m.	Working parties start
12.30	" " stop
2 . .	dinners
5 . .	teas
7.45	Mount sentries etc.

On Wednesday August 5th

1 officer and 32 NCOs & men of the Isle of Wight Rifles arrived to relieve me. The sentries, groups & patrols I have arranged are really very simple, but I thought I never should get this officer to understand them. I imagine it will be all right in a few days.

We got our orders to congregate at Newport that evening. I actually heard that I was to catch the 10.30pm train at 10.45pm! However, we caught it and arrived at Parkhurst about 12.30.

Since then reservists have been pouring in, have been fitted with equipment, boots, clothes etc. etc. and drilled. Late on Friday night we got an order that every man must give up one suit and one pair of boots for Kitchener's 500,000! One would have thought that they could have managed to do this before issuing the clothes. At 11.51 – 9 minutes before our scheduled time – we reported, the Bn [Battalion] mobilised.

Tuesday Aug 11

The last few days have been spent in working up the reservists into some resemblance of soldiers. They are a splendid lot of men, after the boys which comprise a Bn in peace time. Very cheerful and ready to work to the last drop. But at present they have very little discipline, and if things go wrong are apt to give lip to the N.C.Os. Yesterday, we marched down to the Range and sighted the rifles. Most of them shoot extraordinarily well; we did not get back till about four and those left behind had eaten most of the dinners. This was very bad arrangement by the Q.M.S. [Quarter Master Sergeant] I went over luckily to see they were all right and found a regular pandemonium reigning and the N.C.Os absolutely useless. However, I soon had them in hand, and we fed about 30 of them in the canteen.

Today we have been for a 10 mile march, It was intensely hot and a pretty severe test for these fellows. About 60 of them fell out, 3 from my platoon. They stuck it very well for the most part, many I could see were pretty well done. A few days will put this right no doubt. One poor chap I have just heard died soon after they got him home. Still no news of when we are off. Oh how I wish we could get a move on! The

colonel has lectures every day. Extraordinarily clear & interesting; I hope for our sakes he does not get a job; though it will be a monstrous shame if he doesn't.

[Thursday] Aug 13th

Off at last!

Weight stripped	11st 3lbs
Weight full kit	14st 0lbs

Marched to Cowes & on to S Hampton [Southampton] on steamer. Men as pleased as anything to get on the move.

[Friday] Aug 14th

Arrived at [Le] Havre. Some French soldiers on quay gave us a great reception. Our fellows whistled the marches for their benefit, – 1500 whistling together is rather a good show, - and then sang 'Hold your hand out naughty Boy' while the French stood bare headed thinking it was our N.A. [National Anthem]

V. [very] hot, march to rest camp at Harfleur not a great show, discipline wants improving & feet hardening. After a bath & meal war seems better fun than one had anticipated, especially over 200 miles from any enemy. Men recovered spirits as they got their tummies full. French v. [very] kind and rather amusing. I with my insular mind, have laughed v. [very] heartily at them I fear.

[Saturday] Aug 15th

Yesterday blazing hot, not a cloud, today an inch of water and six inches of mud. During the night we had a very severe thunder storm and all day today it has poured. My bivy [bivouac] A.1. until this afternoon, when in my absence a peg came out and I have just wrung half a bucket full of water out of my flea bag. Men cheerful, plenty of grub.

Still raining! O'Donel has just had some orders as to how to keep bicycles & transport in very dry hot weather! We have got a fire going in an old farm house so that we can dry some things.

[Sunday] Aug 16

Still raining this morning. The camp a sea of mud. Transport got off an hour late but considering the mud did v. well. We marched back to .... [blank, assume Le Havre] and entrained by 12. Train left at 3.30. Every station full of people cheering "Les Bon Englais" and loading us with flowers. Many of them seemed to expect to be embraced in return for the flowers, and it would not have been a great hardship sometimes.

At Rouen we stopped and the men had some coffee while the officers had a hurried meal at L'Hotel Moden. I eat more in 5 minutes than I do in one ordinary day and so to bed.

[Tuesday] Aug 18

Bed was not a great success. There were six in the carriage so I slept on the floor & the springs left much to be desired. We arrived in Landrecies about 6 am and marched straight on to Noyelles where we went into billets. We, i.e. Z Coy [Company] have struck a very good patch here. The officers are in a cottage, a little bigger than the other with a most delightful garden full of phloxes. The house is scrupulously clean and contains a feather mattress for all of us. The whole company is within 100x [yards] and we are next door to the mess. My platoon is very snug; all in one house with a little green patch about 20x [yards] square in front, where I have my platoon parades etc. I am very lucky in my platoon, they are a very cheery lot of blighters. The messing is very good, and so is the Vin de Pays I am supprised to find.

Last night produced more weird noises than I have ever heard before. Byng, Attwood, Harding & Cooper sleep in one room and I slept in a broad passage just outside. About 2 am I woke up to hear a lot of gentle little barks followed by the most awful ear splitting yell I have ever heard. This was Harding having a nightmare. I was just dozing after this episode when a bat, which must have been imprisoned under my bed got loose, flapped across my face & fell into a tin can. It rattled round in this making a noise like ten gongs, until I got up and slew it (sent particulars home), and then as I got back to bed the old dame of the house made her noise. She is about 90 and does it all day, but at night it sounds much worse. If a wild cat, mad with rage could clear its throat it would make a noise like this old woman. The country around is undulating and very like

England in places though in most places typically what I expected to find here.

A minute fish was seen in a small pond near by, so about ten persevering soldiers have made themselves rods and lines made out of lengths of cotton from their housewifes [mending kits] and are hard at work hunting it.

[Thursday] Aug 20

The men are most amusing in their efforts to talk the lingo. They make things needlessly hard for themselves by insisting on calling cigarettes "fags" etc. My efforts are not much better. After much thought I can ask for what I want in fairly correct French, but I cannot begin to understand the answer so it does not help much.

Today, we changed billets. I shall never forget Noyelles & the kind old people there. On the whole I think it has been the pleasantest three days soldiering I have ever spent. 3 officers and 10 men might have been seen just now catching ? on ? [illegible] as fast as they could ? out ?? [illegible]

New billets fairly comfortable but not so good as Noyelles. Tomorrow off to the front? Letters seem to be coming in daily now, and I was delighted to get several today and yesterday. Also Pickwick. [by Charles Dickens]

[Friday] Aug 21

Today we were up with the lark, or to be exact 1½ hours before that unpleasant bird, owing to a grogy watch of the sentry. The march today was the longest we have had, though not at all excessive. Men came along A.1. We reached Longueville in good time, Good billets and nice people. The officers of Z Coy had a meal to dream about (I shall never forget), cooked by our hostess, an army contractors wife. Excellent soup, omelettes to dream about, plums, cider & coffee. The French papers I see state that we are within 25 miles of & in the direct line of the main attack of the whole German army. This gives one furiously to think & on the whole seems most satisfactory; my viy! What a funk [panic] I shall be in.

[Saturday] Aug 29

I see my last entry was August 21st but I think it

must have been last year! I cannot write down, say much of what has been happening except personal experiences, because of the danger of it going astray but I can fill all that in later. I don't think I shall forget it! There can be no harm in saying that we had our first scrap at Mons. The Germans must have found it out as we impressed the fact on several hundreds of them. My platoon did not suffer there .... [word obliterated], although they were under long range rifle fire & several shrapnel burst right over them. But the Regiment lost heavily.

Fred Forster, Bowden Smith, Smith, Dease and poor old Joe Mead were all killed. Ashburner wounded & Steele got a black eye. I don't quite know how many men but quite 150. The only event I had was burning a barge. There were 6 of them on the canal we were defending and they were supposed to be burnt. Two did not catch so I went along and got them going. It was not under fire except for the occasional shell and two snipers who hoofed off as soon as I appeared. But I was quite glad when they were blazing.

The people of Mons beat everything in the way of hospitality; eggs, fruit, backy [tobacco], handkerchiefs, in fact everything the men could think of were showered on them. I don't think there was a man in my platoon who cooked less than six eggs. And then we had to retire and leave them to the Germans; it really is a beastly game.

We hear rumours of all sorts of atrocities committed by the Germans. I cannot believe them all but some are indisputable e.g. they undoubtedly got over the bridges by driving women and children before them so that our men could not fire!

[Tuesday] Sept 1
It is now a week since Mons so I can now give some more details. We marched about 20 miles from Longueville arriving at Mons about 12. After waiting about an hour we were sent on to take up an out post possition in front. I had a picket in the most impossible possition on the edge of a wood. I entrenched it & sent out patrols etc. made obstacles and in fact worked hard for about 2 hours. We were then ordered to retire to the canal and put this in a state of defence.

Behind the canal ran a railway, which I had to prepare while Cooper barricaded the bridge. Again the men worked like horses and we did not finish till late that night. Things were made much harder by hundreds of inhabitants coming to feed the men, watch, cross the bridge etc. When all was done we manned the defences & waited. About 10 they started shelling the line, and soon after they burst five or six shell right over one bridge, fortunately hitting no one. This was our first taste of shells; they make a fearful noise and the shrapnel all round is rather alarming but they really do very little damage and as long as the men keep steady there is nothing to get excited about.

Most was my men were A.1. & were soon laughing at it all. Ashburner's company was holding the other main bridge with his coy and this was where the attack came. The whole line was quite indefensible, houses right up to the far bank & no field of fire. They held on most splendidly, however, for a long time, losing 75 out of 200 before they retired in good order. 5 officers, B Smith, Forster, Smith, Dease & Mead were killed here, Ashburner hit & Steele got a black eye. The machine guns were wiped out time after time, but fresh men took their places until the guns were blown to pieces. Finally, we all retired covering the remains of 'B' and 'C' coys. We then marched back a few miles to a large hospital at .... [blank] where we got about four hours sleep at last.

The next morning at about 1 am we were off again to take up a new possition at Ciply. Again we had to take up a far to[o] extended line, with no reserves and no time to make proper trenches. The Germans came on soon after dawn, beginning as usual with the artillery bombardment. Unlike the day before, our artillery was able to answer and a tremendous duel started. We were in support this time just behind the brow of the hill. On the top of the hill there was a house which I had to loop hole with my platoon. We made rather a good job of it I thought & I have since heard that Steele was able to cover the retreat of the firing line from it without losing a man. As soon as this was done our company was sent off to the left flank which the enemy were trying to take. Byng went forward with half the company & took up a possition on the extreme left. The S [South] Lancs were there & if they had only entrenched this possition as they certainly ought, the flank could not have been tamed for at least 2 hours longer.

As it was, Byng was right in the open and had a very hot time from gas, mgs [machine guns] & rifles. He held on there until all the rest of the line had got back and then came back himself covered by my fellows, having lost about 40%. We then all got back together about 21000 yds and waited for the Germans to appear over the crest of the hill. I guessed it to be 1500, and when they did appear opened rapid on them; I saw 5 drop as they reached the crest so the men must have been shooting fairly well. They were still flocking round our left flank so after holding on a little longer we were all ordered to retire & this we managed to do without further losses.

X   X

[Deleted: There then began a long and boring and tiring hike of about 20 miles to ....]

These two delaying actions seem to have been most risky operations and as far as one can see extraordinarily well managed by our generals. We were up against overwhelming force – at Mons our 2 Coys had no less other than 6 Battalions against them! – We expected to be supported by the French & they retired 25 miles the very night before the fight. In a rear guard action the idea is to retire when the enemy are still at long range and here we had to let them get right up to us before we went and got clean away; and this with no resource at all!

This is as far as I may go today with facts.

I had always been under the impression that under fire one would be in a most awful funk [panic] and also that one would be filled with anger at the enemy. This has not been my experience altogether. Of course, it would be ridiculous to say I was not in a funk at first, especially when waiting for it to begin. But we were so busy & tired that I honestly think I was not half so frightened as before the cock house match [a school football match] or army boxing.

When actually under fire, the feeling is entirely one of depression. I wished to goodness it would be soon over, & that one could get rest & grub. It depressed me to see our poor fellows being hit and to hear reports of officers etc and was scarcely less sorry for the Germans I saw wounded than our own fellows. I could not raise any animosity against them although trying my best to kill as many of them as possible. Perhaps an advance & certainly a change would be more inspiriting.

[Thursday] Sept 3

The events from last Tuesday onwards are a complete jumble in my head. I can remember the different places we stopped at, the marches we made & the possitions we took up; also I can remember a pair of very sore feet; but on which day each thing happened the names of the places & distances we marched I have forgotten. Cooper has got all this written down and I will fill in details from him later. Also the battle of Inchy, which I still remember clearly.

X   X   X

On Sept 1 I saw in one field of roots the following coveys of partridges. 1 of 38. 1 of 23. 2 of 9. 1 of 7. 3 of 5 and 3 or 4 of less than 5. Most of them got up within shot & on the 1st of September* it was almost too much!

1st September was, and still is, the beginning of the French hunting season.

+   +   +

Last night we were on out posts again. My platoon was some ¾ mile down a road leading from our billets & over looking Meaux. Just by my picket there was a fairly large house which had just been deserted by its people in such a hurry that nearly all their stuff had been left behind, including any amount of grub. I climbed the wall and systematically looted any perishable stuff that we could make use of, also borrowing some cooking utensils & a <u>bath</u>. So that my platoon had a chicken rabbit & ham stew with vegetables galore, fresh bread & - biggest luxury of all - butter washed down with a little wine & coffee last night & for breakfast this morning. So that what with full tummies & a clean exterior, there was plenty of soap & towels - they are so pleased with themselves that they hardly know what to do.

The country we have been passing through is extraordinarily fine & the best cultivated & most fertile I have ever seen. The roots & wheat are quite extraordinary. The villages are all so picturesque & the farms so solid and comfortable. Although we are so close to Paris there are hardly any modern beastly homes such as there are in England. It seems an awful thing to give up all this lovely country to be burnt & laid waste with hardly a fight.

Last night I got a fresh batch of letters which were very welcome. I had never realised how comforting enjoyment is. Here all we think about is food, drink, sleep & letters & when we get one or more of them one enjoys them as much as the most complicated pleasures at home, e.g. I don't think I ever remember enjoying anything more than my meal, bath & letters last night, although sitting beside a road so dusty with artillery that I could scarcely see across it!

*   *

On Aug 24th we fell back from the position behind Mons at about 9 am. We were rear guard and marched steadily back, taking up a possition now and again until 11.30, when we reached Bermeries having covered ..... [blank, probably about 20] miles. Here we got about 5 hours sleep which were very welcome, my feet were rather sore and I had started a chafe.

We were off again next morning by 5 am and we marched straight away to Inchy a distance of about 35 miles. We halted on the near side of Inchy just as it started to pour with rain, and then to put the lid on it we were taken for out posts. This was the worst day we have had at all: for some time I had been having a job to get along at all, what with my feet & chafe and the men were dead beat. However, 'D' Coy were not taken for out posts after all, they were only in support, so we did get some sleep in. Also I got my boots off for the first time for 6 days and managed to buy a pair of socks & some boracid powder after which I was a new man.

At dawn of the 26th we moved back through Inchy and took up an extended possition behind it at Cambrai. We dug trenches frantically for a short time, but there were not enough tools and no facilities for overhead cover & very little time. When we had done

what we could the 5th relieved us in the trenches & we were ordered back in support. By this time, the artillery duel was in full swing. Behind the possition was a little sunken lane running parallel with the possition and just as we were getting back to this a hail of shell burst right over the battalion; my platoon was sitting down just by the lane, and the first shell knock over five men and punctured my water bottle. We then doubled about 20 yds into the lane where there was a good deal of confusion, and on the right there was a short panic before the officers got the men under control. I am glad to say my platoon did not get out of control at all.

We then lay in that lane all day, quite snug. Pellets of all sorts whistled over our heads but down in there was practically no danger & we were able to cook & eat a hot meal. Our guns pounded away hour after hour and in front the rifle fire kept going pretty steadily. At about 1 there was a lull in the firing and we all thought we had beaten them off. Suddenly they opened a tremendous burst of firing in the centre of the line to our right. All their guns seemed to be concentrated on a village that was there, and about 3.30 the order came for a general retirement.

Then I saw a sight I hope never to see again. Our line of retreat was down two roads which converged to a Village about a mile behind the possition. Down these roads came a mob. Men from every regiment were there, guns riderless horses, limbers packed with wounded, quite unattended & lying on each other, jolting over ruts etc. It was not a rout, only complete confusion. This was the Germans chance.

One battery of artillery sent forward or one squadron of cavalry would have turned this rabble into a complete rout and the whole Army would have been dispersed & cut up piece meal. Meanwhile we were the only Rt [regiment] I saw in any order. We had not been engaged and had only lost one officer, (Sampson hit in the stomach) and about 30 men; we had also had a hot meal so that we were in good condition.

When the retirement was ordered we went back in a succession of extended lines in absolute order & formed up behind a farm house near where the roads met. Here we waited in mass while the remains of the army streamed past. It was a most trying ½ hour. It seemed inevitable that they would follow up & then the jam in that village would have been indescribable. I have since heard they had sustained fearful losses & also a division of French cavalry was covering our retreat.

When the rabble had gone past we moved off, marching at attention, arms sloped, fours dressed etc. through the Village. By this time the rest of the brigade had formed up and we took up a covering possition behind the Village, which we hung onto expecting an attack any moment. But it never came and about 7 pm we moved off again and marched till 12pm. I believe we got a good mark for this show from Smith-D[orrien] & Hamilton. Of course we had no reason to lose our formation, but a panic is very catching & there is no doubt that at one time we were the only troops who could have put up any show at all.

I have since heard that the 5th Div [Division] lost 60 guns & several regiments were practically wiped out. The Cheshires were only 200 men & 5 officers before the battle! Also I fear two regiments ran very fast when they might have held on & so broke the line.

At 2 am on the 27th we were on the march again fetching up at Hargincourt at 9.30 where we had a short rest and some food. My chafe is practically alright now & my feet improving. At 11 we went on rear guard again. We seem to be perpetually rear guard! It is hard work but I suppose we have suffered less than most people. At 7 pm we reached Vermand where there was a small ration of tea for the men who needed it badly.

At midnight we were off again with the promise of rest when we had put a river behind us. We reached Ham at 9.30 & as usual the RFs [Royal Fusiliers] took up the covering position which we hung on to until the 4th D [Division] had crossed away on our right. At 1 pm we marched off again reaching Crisolles at 7 pm. This was a most trying march after all we had done during the week, and over these damnable paving stones; & I must say our fellows, most especially the company did splendidly. D trudged along with their fours covered etc & hardly a

man fell out & though I says it they were 50% better than any other coy. At Crisolles we did at last get a good rest & even a better meal.

The next morning we loafed about & rested all morning until 1 pm when we went forward – rear guard again – and took up a possition along the front edge of a large forest. There were several Uhlan [German cavalry] patrols about who we were able to fire at occasionally & they burst some shell rather unpleasantly near. At dusk we retired for 5 miles through the wood. The path was only a narrow track & very rough & in places ankle deep in mud, and as they went at a great pace we were very glad to halt at Noyon where a kind old soul made us a meal. After a short halt we went on to Cuts where we arrived at 1.30 am where we had a short "poss" until 4.30 am and so on to Vic Sur Aisne which we reached at 7 am. Here we had a good rest & feed, also some letters, letters are one of the three great Events. Food & Sleep being the other two.

My feet & chafe are O.K. now & I am getting as strong as a horse at first one shoulder used to get rather tired with my load. Now I have nearly doubled the load and I don't feel it. I can keep going all day quite happily & if necessary most of the night. Most of the men are very fit too. I would much rather go into action with the 20 men I have left than the 59 I started with as I can trust all of them to the last inch now & before this war some serious shirkers & many unfit.

I marched out with 59. Of those 8 have been taken off jobs; 5 to other platoons; 4 sent back sick; 8 known to be wounded and 9 are missing.

We left Vic Sur Aisne at 7 am on the morning of the 31st and legged it to Vaumoise where we had rather uncomfortable and buggy billets in a suggar factory. We got in there at 5.30 pm and next morning at 6.30am went forward & took up an out post possition. Leaving

X   X   X

Vaumoise we were again rear guard to the Bde until we reached Bouillancy at about 9 pm. Here we stopped in billets until 5 am on the 2nd when we went on to Penchard where we arrived at 2.30 and Z Coy were out posts for the Bde.

+   +   +

Leaving here at 6.30 we arrived at Le Ferme du Mons marching through the Foret de Mons. Here we billeted in a large farm where we got any amount of Eggs, Milk, Fresh Cheese and Butter, also a lot of unripe fruit which I eat a surfeit of with the usual unpleasant results.

We took up a position S [south] of this farm and at about 11 pm set out on a very trying night march to Chatres, arriving there about 7 am, rather exhausted. Here we stayed till Sunday morning.

[Sunday] Sept 6th

When we actually Advanced. Needless to say we were advanced guard and after many halts & changes of direction we fetched up at Lumigny at 7 where we billeted. Here we are getting all sorts of rumours. It seems certain that we & the French are going to assume the offensive & if reports are true we have got the Germans in a very tight place. I am not belligerent by nature but after all this retiring day after day I should have to actually advance and have a dip at them. As far as one can tell their musketry is beneath contempt, their artillery is well handled, but the shrapnel seems to do very little executing. The Cavalry say their cavalry is no good at shock tactics and is very fond of dismounted action when they are handicapped by their rotten mortality. Reports say their horses are stone cold, their guns worn out and their men very short of food. I wonder!

[Tuesday] Sept 8

We remained at Lumigny all yesterday morning moving on again at about 1. The officers cooked a hot meal at about 12 Bacon, bully beef and some potato chips which I produced. Again we advanced, and for the first time saw remains of German trenches, billets etc. & nearly 40 dead horses. We passed through Coulommiers at about 5 pm, which had only been evacuated by the Germans that morning & yet they had got the trains running already and we picked up our second reinforcements.

These bring my platoon up to full strength again.

We reached La Bretonniere at about 8 pm where we bivouacked for the night & all had a lot of rum. One thing this campaign has done for me is to give me a taste for most sorts of alcohol including Vin de Pays, cognac, Eau de Vie, rum, cider & port. I found some straw in a loft where the Germans had been sleeping & I made a bed out of this in our field. I woke up in the morning having scratched myself into a rash all over & wondering if I had got some foul disease or if I had not been alone in my bed. Both conjectures were right, the disease might be called German Measles and I have just caught 3 of the aforesaid measles in my shirt.

We have had great news of a French victory on our right & as I write all three of our divisions are pounding away at the flank of a German Army Corps which we believe to be being followed by the French on the right, & to be going to be cut off by more French on our left. Meanwhile, we are in reserve, a very gentlemanly position to be in!

One realizes more and more on this sort of show ones own feelings & moods are purely reactions of the stomach. If I have 8 meals a day then for 8 hours at least during that day everything seems rosy. If I go short of food for a day no rumour is too gloomy to be true. A little brandy makes me think of home and the extreme probability of being there within a week, - a very little will have this result and last night my tot of rum made me feel quite poetical and a smoky fire that smelt abominably of burnt bacon fat seemed to be quite a romantic camp fire. Just now I am well fed & happy.

We are sitting in a corn field, while the Germans are shelling the road which the Germans believe us to be on. They are holding a possition on the opposite side of the hill. They held us up for some time in that possition but we were not brought into the firing line to turn them out going on through there we bivouacked in a field behind an old cement factory at Vauciennes. Here I was as sick as a dog.

The next morning we started again at day break; before we had been going long two of our guns came into action against the flank of two of the enemy's guns and put them out of action in less than no time. This was very interesting as we could see the whole show through our glasses. The next place we were stopped at was a wood at Marigny.

There were two German batteries and two machine guns & some infantry here. The Lincolns - , again got at the guns from the flank, and the gunners destroyed 4 before leaving them. They then made a counter attack & drove our people out of it. By this time, the 5th Dn [Division] had come up on our left and there was some very heavy firing in the wood which went on for the rest of the day. Our guns dropped a bit of shell into the wood & I believe hit a lot of our own fellows. At dark the firing stopped & we remained in our trenches as battle out posts all night, a most wearisome job.

During the night one of our patrols was fired on and 2 men in our company were hit. I am fairly certain it was our own men who did this as I believe the Germans all cleared off at dusk. The next morning was as dismal a one as I can remember. We were all rather tired after the out posts, & owing to some orders miscarrying, we had no time for grub; & to put a lid on it, it began to rain steadily cold sort of drizzle. At about 9 am we halted for a short time when news came in from the Cavalry that the Germans were having breakfast a short way ahead. The R.7. were van guard so off we went as hard as we could go. After about 2 miles we came round a corner and saw on the opposite side of the valley a long convoy of German baggage winding slowly up the hill. We entrenched at once & doubled down into the village of Vinly in the valley. Here we were under cover & reformed.

By this time the guns were in action pounding away at the convoy & its guard. Steele's platoon entrenched & came into the firing line fast & I entrenched mine and made them lie down just behind the brow of the hill ready to reinforce. We soon got the order & doubled as hard as we could pelt over a stubble field to line a bank beyond Steele's platoon. As soon as we showed we were met by a long way the hottest fire I have seen. The enemy were lining the edge of a wood in the valley below us at about 400 [yards] and they let us have it with rifle & machine gun the whole way across that field. The ground was churned up all round us & how we only lost 3 men I can't imagine. I got one pellet through the put[t]ee

[*cloth strip wound round the lower leg*]. When we reached the bank, things were rather better as we could keep their fire down with our own. But it was a bad possition as we were plumb on the skyline & they had excellent cover in the wood.

The machine gun was soon put out of action, however, & then we gradually got superiority of fire. I had 150 steady carefully aimed shots at pink faces in the wood at 400 [yards] & if I did no execution I am a Dutchman. Meanwhile things were getting rather warm for us all & especially for me personally as owing to my having to have my head up the whole time searching for targets with my glasses they soon were able to track me down as an officer. At least so I believe, though no doubt I am a prejudiced party. At any rate I had one pellet through the sleeve, one through my revolver holster one all down my side & four or five which got mud all over me. This was all most exciting and being able to see the enemy & fire at them makes all the difference. I really rather enjoyed it.

Finally I got a pellet through the fleshy part of the arm. Rather painful at the time, but only quite a simple flesh wound not hitting a bone, artery or anything. By time I had got it tyed up they had surrendered & we were able to close on the road. Once one is in the firing line one cannot tell what is happening elsewhere any more than if you were a 100 miles away, but I gather what happened was this. We surprised a convoy with its guard before they could take up a possition. Their guns & cavalry cleared off at once & the infantry, 4 bns [battalions] were left behind to let the baggage escape.

These were practically surrounded & killed in large number and captured I believe about 1500. Most of the baggage escaped with the exception of 12 waggons which the artillery bagged. This is the first real victory we have had. Of course we were in overwhelming numbers, but still it was a victory. My platoon had 1 NCO and 1 man killed. 1 officer, 2 NCOs and 4 men wounded, total 9. We then went on a short way to billets at Dammard, where I had my arm properly dressed.

The next day Sept 11 I started off with the Bn but the M.O. [Medical Officer] got me back to the ambulance after we had gone a mile. Of course I can march as well as ever, but just at present for a few days I could not go into the firing line, so I am inefficient & must go back to rail head. This is annoying as I feel such a humbug but I suppose can't be helped. I trecked along with the cadets all day & bivouacked with them last night at ...... [blank] & I believe we shall be sent back today.

I don't know what our losses were but 4 officers were hit. Tower, v. badly just below the heart, but I am told he may survive. Beazley twice in the leg, Jackson in the head & really sick. Also 2 officers are sick, so we are getting v. short.

Notes

There are a few things I have forgotten to mention. We have seen several air fights & they are the most fascinating thing to watch. In each case the German was the slower machine and our own or the Frenchman as the case might be came circling round & round, now working its way above & now dipping right down at it as if it were going to ram it, then checking & we could hear faint little bangs as they fired at each other with their revolvers. One day, I can't remember which, we had been watching one of these fights & the German had got clean away by dropping down very low. This brought him over us at a height of about 1500 feet when the whole Bn, which was in column of rout opened rapid on him and down he came. They managed the plane to the ground and before our people could get there had burnt the aeroplane & escaped into the wood. I never heard if they were caught.

I shall be very glad to see my 35lbs kit again. It is 12 days now since I changed my underclothing & socks & my boots are nearly done in. The last few days I have been rather seedy. Head aches & bilious, also an annoying rash & one or two of my silly old fainting fits. But a little blood letting seems to have done me a lot of good and a day or two rest no doubt will put me right again.

[Sunday] Sept 13th

Yesterday was the most wretched day I have ever spent I think. There are five of us with the ambulance. Whiney and Barton & Brown of the R.S.F. [Royal Scots Fusiliers] sick, Jackson & myself

wounded. We were expecting to go to rail head the night before last & hourly afterwards. So all day yesterday we were in that beastly ambulance. It was infernally cold & raining cats and dogs, and for real discomfort give me an ambulance wagon.

We started at about 5 & we did not get in until 12 when we reached Braine. All the time we could hear guns & I felt an awful humbug not to be with the regiment.

When we got here we went into billets in a large house that had been ransacked by the Germans. I must say this has been rather an eye opener. I have never seen such an incompetent casual lot as the RAMC [Royal Army Medical Corps] officers or such an undisciplined rabble as their men are.

To take one example, which did not matter but which might have been serious. On the morning of Sept 11 Jackson & I came in with notes to have our wounds examined for splinters. On the afternoon of the 12th as no one had been near us we heaved round a bit & at last got a corporal to dress us! And this, not because they were busy as no wounded came in during all that time. When we reached Braine at 12 o'clock at night in the pouring rain they all, officers & men made straight off into billets and would have left us in that damnable waggon not ever knowing that we were not going on further. However, this morning we were shipped off to a French hospital & here at last I have been able to be of use.

It is quite a small place & absolutely chock full of wounded, chiefly Germans. So Jackson & I went off to get houses, beds, straw etc for as many as possible. I got two good houses one with four beds. This I turned into an officers "ward". We all packed in here & then I rescued two cavalry officers who were wedged in among the Germans, & later two more turned up. Then we went & bought quantities of vegetables of all sorts & brought them along & at present I am making a stew out of bully, potatoes, carrots and onions. We expect to go back to rail head tonight. The sister here is a most wonderful person. She talks French, German and English fluently, runs the hospital, feeds the patients & in fact does everything. I hope to be back in a day or two now.

[Monday] Sept 14th

Still in Braine. I think I should make a very good hospital nurse. There are two fellows next door with broken arms & I can dress and undress them in record time now. The stew was a great success. I added a lot of hot water & made some excellent soup for the invalids, which was about the first food they had been able to eat. Today they had a look at my arm and said I could go back tomorrow afternoon and it would probably be fit to use the next day. About five minutes later I got another message that we were all to go down to rail head after all. This is awful nonsense as I feel quite fit to go into the firing line now. The guns are still pooping away ahead. This is the 23rd consecutive day our people have been in action.

There is a young M.O. [Medical Officer] here in charge of this hospital who is doing exceedingly well, and seems to be working day & night as far as I can make out from his signature. His name is O'Rook. Looking back I seem to have put myself down for a great lot of diseases all at once. I can't say I felt half as bad as the list looks. Yesterday I had a wash all over & a shave, a kind inhabitant supplyed me with some Eau de Cologne which did my rash a lot of good & was very refreshing. I am rather anxious about the 9th Bde and wish to goodness I was with them. As far as one can hear they crossed the Aisne last night & then the German guns blew up the bridges behind them before the rest of the division could cross. If it is anything more than a rear guard action they are in a very critical possition. We have just heard however that the French are over at Soissons and our left wing are over so I expect it is all right.

These French men are blood thirsty little swine. When I was going round getting rooms for hospitals, they all made it quite clear that if we brought any wounded Germans there they would cut their throats; this they illustrated with much accuracy & the keenest enjoyment. I hear that two inhabitants had to be shot this morning for knifing two wounded Germans. This is in great contrast to our fellows, who as soon as they have caught a German seem to do nothing but feed him with their own rations. Of course the cases are very different, for the French have had their country invaded and are told that the Germans are committing every sort of atrocity. Of course this is not true but there is no doubt that they ransack & destroy all private property they find in the houses as we have invariably found to our own discomfort.

[Tuesday] Sept 15th

We did get off in the motor lorries after all yesterday. There were 10 wounded officers in our lorry, and we were packed fairly close. We put down a lot of straw so it was comfortable enough for the less bad cases but the jolting was very bad for fractures and as one daren't move hand or limb for fear of hurting someone it was not an enjoyable journey. We started at 4 and reached Breny at about 6. Here I expected to remain a day or two & so back again, but not a bit of it! In spite of several very heavy protests back we have to go to ...... [*erased*] about 200 miles back & this without anyone looking to see if I was wounded at all. As soon as I get there I suppose I shall change trains and come back again.

Of course this is all very nice & peaceful & I hope to be able to get a bath & some clean clothes at .... [*erased*]. If only I had more excuse for it all I wouldn't mind, but as it is I do feel a humbug.

This seems a good opportunity to send this back. I don't suppose any one in the world could read it but myself, but some of it may be decipherable & in any case it is so much the less to carry, so I will try to get it off if I can.

Sunday Sept 20

I rather forget how far I got in my journal, but I don't think I had written up Le Mans at all. We arrived at the station at about 8.30pm on Tuesday Sept 15th. We all bundled out of the train onto the platform where we remained for 2 hours & a half, presumably while the R.A.M.C. [Royal Army Medical Corps] staff had their dinner. Then we were put into a motor ambulance and driven to some artillery barracks which had been fitted up as a "rest camp for stragglers" of all sorts and very slightly wounded. Here we were told we were not wanted, so we went off and took rooms in a hotel.

After a great deal of talk – which I had to do – we managed to get a meal of bread & cheese & so to bed. The next day we reported at the rest camp at 10.30 & again at 2.30 when we were sent to the Base

Commandant. He told us we ought never to have been taken to the rest camp but to one of the two hospitals & that we were to be examined there the following morning. Having at last found out what was expected of us we took ourselves off and had a real good bath and shave. This was A1. It was the first bath that I have had since I have been in France! We then set about refitting.

Le Mans is quite a large place with plenty of good shops & a large church, or perhaps it is a cathedral? This stands up well on the hill and appears to be rather a fine place but spoilt by having been very heavily buttressed at some time or other. First of all I refitted myself with under clothing and then feeling the complete little gentleman again. I laid in stores for the coy [company] mess, when I returned potted meats, chocolate, matches, cigarettes, candles, razor blades etc. etc. I have protested against being sent here till I am sick of it & am doing all I can to be sent back at once, but in the meanwhile I intend to make the most of this little spell of civilisation.

The Hotel de France is not good really but it seems the acme of comfort at present and there is a capital restaurant next door where we have our cafe au lait at odd times & dinner in the evening. The town is full of English officers of the very queerest description. R.A.M.C. [Royal Army Medical Corps], A.O.C. [Army Ordinance Corps], A.V.C. [Army Veterinary Corps], A.S.C. [Army Service Corps] and Special Reserve reinforcements of all sorts. Hardly any of them can talk Kings English and most of them are too important to be civil. It would have done me a lot of good to have had a turn up with one or two of them. I hope the French don't think they are the typical English officer.

The next morning we reported at a hospital, No 5. Here there was a fussy little Major who looked at our wounds and in removing the bandage removed the scab also. Then noticing it was not healed underneath he said we must wait another 3 or 4 days and offered to send us to a chateau belonging to an American millionaire nearby, who was putting up convalescent British officers. I knew that would mean hanging about for weeks so we refused his kind offer & escaping without being given our names we tried hospital No 1 where they passed us fit without even

looking at the wounds. We reported thus at the BCs [Battery Commander] office and then continued refitting. In the afternoon we motored to the A.O. [Area of Operations] store about 3 miles out where we made up some deficiencies in military kit & I managed to loot a large bath bag to put all my stuff in.

That evening we got orders to report the next morning at the rest camp for duty & to be ready to start at a moments notice. We reported soon after 8 & were turned on to censor letters. There was an accumulation ten days old and though 3 of us put in 7½ solid hours at it we did not make much impression. It was quite an education to read these letters: most of them follow the same lines, but every type of fellow was there. There were some typical mob orators, who wrote about the "gallant boys" & "British grit" etc. Then there was the grouser, the backstick, (in large numbers) the wag & the sickly sentimental in greatest profusion. I was rather despairing at first as one was so sorry for the poor devils, who have been chucked out here away from their families & jobs to fight in a cause they don't care two pins about. After a bit one skimmed through the letters without reading anything but censorable stuff.

When we left at 6 pm they told us we were off by a train at 2.30 am that night, so we had an early dinner and put in about 4 hours sleep, and about 3 am we actually started off! I have thoroughly enjoyed my little holiday at Le Mans, but I am glad to be going back again to muck in with the rest of them again. I forgot to say that Whiney, who has been having a very bad time with malaise and toothache was kept at the hospital & I expect will be sent home. He says he will return in two days but I doubt it. Barton got separated from us but I hear he is rather bad & certainly ought to go home. He should never have been passed fit. Who should I meet on the train but James Gunnell! He is coming up with his first reinforcements & is in great form. The train pegs along at about 10 miles per hour stopping 10 minutes or so at every station.

When we shall get back, goodness knows. At Versailles we met a train load of our wounded going down to the base. Jacko poor chap heard that his brother had been killed, and I found one of our own fellows who told me Attwood & Cole were dead &

Byng wounded; I hope to goodness this is not true, but I fear it must be. This has left us all very depressed. At Villeneave we came up with a whole lot of trains full of reinforcements, both French & English & here we had to stay all night, starting on our snails crawl again at 6 am the next morning. Meanwhile, the big battle is going on all the time & we have only ten officers left at the very most.

Wednesday Sept 23

We arrived at Braisnes, or rather just outside it, at about 8 am on the 21st, having been in the train 54 hours. Here we herded all the nondescripts into a field and got them sorted out into Bdes. I was detailed to return the 8th Bde scallywags to their Bde. They were in the trenches about 5 miles in front of Braine in front of the River Aisne. The bridge over the Aisne had been blown up, and they had made a pontoon bridge in its place which the enemy could observe and shelled whenever troops crossed over. So I could not start till after dark when I was ordered to join the supply train.

Meanwhile we heard that the Fusiliers had been relieved from the trenches and were bivouacked in a village 2 miles off. So as I feared I have missed this show. As soon as I had made the necessary arrangements I hared off to find our fellows. I soon found them and it was quite like getting home again. The officer is not a demonstrative bird, but the men in my platoon had the good taste to pretend they were pleased to see me! The news I heard was only too true. Byng was known to be dead, Cole, Attwood & Hobbs almost certainly dead, Ored & Hughes wounded. Poor old Byng!

I am sorry about him; He was such a nice old thing. I have been in his company since I joined, and he has always been the best of Company Commanders, being kind in unobtrusive little ways, and pretending to be as grumpy as anything when found out. And I know no one who could make more of a good, or even a moderate story. He was not a brilliant officer, and on manoeuvres at home seldom failed to make a hash of the situation whatever it might be; But under the hottest fire he was much cooler than in peace time and the men all loved him, which is the most important thing for regimental officers.

As far as I can make out this is what the Regiment have done since I have been away. On the Saturday after I left them, they pushed on over the Aisne and again were sent on too far. During the night they took up a possition at the apex of a salient in the line. When daylight came the German's main possition was right opposite them and they opened a fearfull fire on them. Shells, m.g. [machine guns] and rifle fire as usual. They hung on for some time but received no support from regiments on each flank and after loosing very heavily were ordered to retire. They then entrenched a possition in the general line where they hung on for eight days, being attacked constantly day & night. When they were relieved on Monday they had not lost an inch of ground for a moment in any part of their line. French, Smith D [Dorrien], Hamilton & Shaw all personally congratulated them all after, & I believe every one are very pleased with the Rgt. All this of course I missed!

Meanwhile I returned to my scallywags and marched them off to their owners. They were not shelling the bridge though there was a lot of very heavy firing going on all along the line, and a few pellets were coming over when we got to the Village. There were two Bns retiring over the hedge – the other two Bns of our Bde who had been relieved by the 17th Bde. There were the 2 bns relieving them; there was a stream of wounded, & a counter stream of empty stretchers, & finally the supply & ammunition columns. All these were trying to get along the road and over the bridge; it was pitch dark and I had the devil of a job not to loose my scallywags. Only two Gordon's [Gordon Highlanders] escaped me. I then biked back & got to our billets at 12 pm.

[Thursday] Sept 24th

Since my last entry we have remained here in billets resting. Cooper is in Command of the Company and I am second in command at present. I am very disgusted with the state of my platoon. When I left they were the cheeriest and my opinion the best disciplined platoon of the lot (perhaps I may be prejudiced). Just before I left Sgt Kite came out from the Depot & was left in charge as he still is. He appears to be quite useless and has let them run absolutely to seed.

Since I have been here I have had several letters

and parcels which are all very welcome. At present as there are 20 few officers left (5 head gunners and 9 Company officers, counting 3 new reinforcements) head gunners mess together and the Rgtl [Regimental] officers in another mess, I am Judas to this mess and Steele, Cooper & I all forage for supplies. After my rest at Le Mans food does not seem to be of such overwhelming importance. Our billet is over the bakery. This is useful as far as getting bread is concerned, but as a queue forms in the street outside our windows at 5 am and they chatter like a combination of indignant monkeys and ravaging wolves until 7.30. I wish it was somewhere, where the bread would bake even quicker.

A short way up the road between here and Braine there have been some aeroplane guns, which poop off furiously whenever a German aeroplane appears. We can see the shell bursts, but the aeroplanes are too far. I wonder if any have been hit.

It is getting very cold at nights & I am mighty glad we are in billets: this morning all the kits of officer casualties were opened, letters and Valuables sent home and anything of use shared amongst us and the men. I secured a flask and a couple of warm vests, so for the present at any rate I have nothing to fear from the cold. But one realises that something must be done for the winter, so I sent off a rather involved letter home for winter uniform. The weather is perfect again. This morning felt just like the best sort of September morning at home & one could almost smell partridges. I proposed starting with Peascroft and Watchcroft over the road. The slight W [west] wind ought to take them over the top end of Sacombe, then the Sacombe Bourne drive and Sacombe Ley over the top end of the Malm Bourne. (I fear the Peas and Watch croft birds will go back.) Then the Malms and red tin barn field and lunch at the R.T.B. After lunch Frogs Hall etc and back by Standon fields.

Bag 57 brace, 13 hares, 3 pigeons, 1 plover. But we drivel

[The above are all names of fields in Braughing]

[Friday] Sept 25th

We are up & off today back to the trenches. Of course this is all very hearthy [hearty] but in some ways I am glad as I shall have a go at the biggest battle of the war so far. We return over the bridge after dark as usual.

[Saturday] Sept 26

Here we are at the trenches. As a matter of fact I am in very comfortable billets, and but for the fact that they are dropping shell about the place, we could be very ~~comfortable~~ happy. Z Coy is in reserve, the other three Coys being actually in the trenches. Our possition is at the top of a hill above Vailly and is very well entrenched, so the people there as far as shell fire goes are much safer than we are as we are only hiding behind walls; but I fear they are not so comfortable and it must be deuced cold at nights.

This house is an A.1. place. Bath room! with a stove to it! Beds, a kitchen range & a nice old caretaker who is as hospitable as she can be. She is rather a superior old thing who might well own the house & she comes in and has meals with us. Cooper and I found the place but we thought we ought to let head quarters know about it so they have come and taken possetion [possession]. Of course we are only too pleased to have the Colonel and O'Donel but the Major is really rather a tiresome little man, perpetually fussing round.

I see I forgot to note the aeroplane bomb. Two were dropped into our billets, one right through a roof of our company billets but no one was seriously damaged. I don't think they were meant for us, but it was one trying to drop bombs on another.

[Sunday] Sept 27

In the trenches propper. Last night I took over Steele's Coy as he was seedy. I am now the next on the list for a company! The possitions were very simple and as I had two subalterns [subordinates] I got some sleep, thanks to my Shetland woolley.

This morning Cooper and Z Coy relieved Steele's Coy and I joined Cooper; so here we all are curled up like beans in our own little bomb proof holes. I hope to goodness they are bomb proof as they are shelling us as I write. They are treating us to a little high explosive shell as a small chunk has just descended gently into my shelter. It shall be kept. Things are getting rather warm each of these blessed shell covers one with sand and shakes the whole place. The danger is very slight but they do put the wind up me more than any amount of rifle fire. I am rather disgusted with the state of my nerves since I came back from the base. I suppose being hit, however slightly is rather a shock and they certainly are not as good as they were before. I am not afraid of finding myself bolting one fine day, but these blessed shells make me blink & bob and I hear imaginary ones at night if anyone snores too loud. I wonder if other people are the same. I hope so. Meanwhile my more pressing danger is of being stung by a wasp, as there are 3 or 4 dozen or so buzzing round me trying to filch my jam. I imagine they are trying to counteract the shell on the counter imitation principle.

[Thursday] October 1

Since my last entry nothing of any great importance has happened. I started improving my hole on the 27th and by the time I was relieved on the 29th it was a regular palace. Cup, bowls, 1 table and 2 chairs made out of ration boxes & a convenient shell fragment for a hammer. A wash hand stand with mirror compleat [tin lining of ammunition box with polished lid] steps up & down etc. etc. In fact I had the chance of playing "Huts" again & keeping my dignity. Percy & Algernon, the heavy and field guns only shell us occasionally now and our casualties since we have been up here are 5.0.0.3. This is due to the excellence of our shelters. On the 29th, X Coy relieved us and we went back into reserve for a day & nights rest. This was very welcome, as we got really warmed at a fire and then a sleep in bed between sheets – with clothes on – which I needed. I should like to describe the possition with a plan, but I suppose it won't do. But the first line & second line, the alternative possitions, the day & night possitions, possitions for bringing guns and converging fire would all be very interesting afterwards & I could not write it from memory. If the Bn is relieved I will chance it while it is fresh in my mind.

I heard yesterday that I had been reported missing at home. This is too bad! As if people did not have enough to worry about without careless mistakes by some blasted W.O. [War Office] clerk. I have also had a lot of letters and parcels from HAL, CJL, SL, ML, MM, SM and MJ [family and friends – see letters chapter] so I am doing fine. Today we relieved W in a

new possition close to our old one & I have been with a look out post all day. Very quiet, no shell near except some shrapnel meant for an aeroplane and only a few snipers.

[Sunday] Oct 4

On the 2nd I got some more letters & some caramels. For some reason every one seems to have a craving for sweet stuff. Jam is by far the most popular of our rations, and any grub that arrives is disposed of before you can say "knife". I was quite the most important man of the day with my caramels; all the officers kept dropping in during the day to see if I had seen anything from my look out post. That evening we were relieved by the Buffs [Royal East Kent Regiment] and made a long night treck [trek] to Servenay a distance of about 16 miles. We left Vailly at 7 pm arriving at our billets in a huge farm at 2.30 am.

These farms in this part of France make our little homesteads in England look rather foolish. This particular one accommodated 800 men, the officers, transport, forces etc. without any trouble. The country we marched over was the most sparsely populated we have seen. We covered most of ten miles without seeing a home of any kind, nothing but acres of mangle & corn stubbles. At Servenay I got a large budget of letters, papers etc. & was glad to hear that the first part of my journal had arrived. We have been taking the general precautions not to be observed by aeroplanes. No doubt we are preparing some surprise stroke on the left flank but what exactly no one knows.

That evening we were off again at 6 pm marching to Troesnes where we arrived at about 12 midnight at another of these big farms, though this time not nearly so nice. It is partly occupied by some French Territorials, also a Scotch Regiment was here the night before. So the result is uncleanly, and bare of all sorts of food stuffs. Also I had an encounter with a kilted bug in my apology for a bed. There were rather too many stragglers from the march last night, and this is due almost entirely to the state of the men's feet. During the long marches of the retreat all our feet got thoroughly bruised right through the soles and then hardened. When we stopped marching for 3 weeks the men hardly used their feet but also seldom were able to get their boots off. The result of all this in my case at any rate that at first my feet became absolutely numbed and feelingless, and when I started marching again became exceedingly sore. In fact at present they are much worse than they have been since we have been out here.

[Tuesday] Oct 6

Off again at 6 pm, and another long march. Just as we started O'Donel told me that I had been detailed to do a job of work as R.T.O. [Railway Transport Officer] and I was to report myself at Div H.Q. at 7 am. We reached .... [left blank, possibly Crepy] at 3 am and there I was greeted by the news that I must report at 5 am instead of 7. This did not leave much time for sleep! When we got there, Jackson, 4 NCOs and 6 men & self – Jackson & the others were sent to Le Meux in a Motte Ambulance [this was the first main ambulance station], which was to be our station, whilst I and the representatives of the 4 other Rgts in the Bde, went like lords in a car to the Corps head Q. [Quarters]. Here we got our orders and an excellent breakfast – Buttery eggs, bacon, coffee, milk & butter & honey - . Then we motored comfortably on to our stations. When I got to mine I found that some other branch I.G.C. [Inspector-General of Communications] or something had already sent a Major & full subaltern as R.T.Os for Le Meux, so after mucking round & helping them for a bit, & got outside another enormous meal we turned in & slept for about 12 hours. The next morning we got our orders to rejoin our regiments, and departed by train at about 4 pm. We took over from the Major later during the morning and as we caught up 4 hours of the 3 he had lost I think we justified ourselves.

[Wednesday] Oct 7

We were told that the journey would take at least 24 hours but at 4 am today I woke up to find we had arrived. I tumbled the men out and got them curled up in some straw until daylight. Then we left them there and went in search of Div Head Qtrs. The town we found to be Abbeville, and Div H.Qrs needless to say were at the most comfortable hotel. Here we discovered the billeting area of the Bn & when we had again breakfasted at length and when I had purchased a hamper of supplies for the mess we came on here.

No one here knew where anything was and it was

not till about 3 that we heard the exact whereabouts of our billets and here I still am waiting for some conveyance for my precious hamper.

[Thursday] Oct 8th

Yesterday I spent a happy day at a little wayside cafe in La Grand Laviers. We got there at about 12 and I and my hamper were the last to leave in a country cart at about 7 pm. Abbeville is a good sized town with plenty of shops and I wish I had more time to spend there to get some woolly clothes. I did try for some pants but they had nothing possible & I shall have to write for them. The church has a very fine front with a v. nice old carved door, which pleased me very much. I just had time to look inside but was again disappointed with the interior. I do not like these gaudily painted images etc at all and one misses the tombs & monuments one would expect to find in English churches of the same date. Perhaps, I have been unlucky in my choice of churches. Talking of churches, the only thing the Germans have done yet which to my mind will allow of no explanations & excuses is the destruction of Rheims. It really seems almost inconceivable that any one with any pretension to civilisation would do a thing like that!

At Laviers there was a very kind old thing with a daughter who told me that she talked English. She may have – probably did – but I could not detect it. They were very nice to me, however, and insisted on my having all my meals with them (they live at Paris & were only staying there) and when I departed we exchanged addresses & I was made to promise to write to her for anything I wanted.

Today, we are in very comfortable billets at Builly [probably Buigny]. I have acquired a bed and a nice old soul who brings me a huge bole [bowl] of chocolate in the morning. It is a tiny cottage; scrupulously clean, but evidently belonging to very poor people. All the cottages here have open hearths with no conveniences for cooking except a spit & tripod; where we have been before they have always had good cooking ranges.

I hear we are to be reinforced by 9 officers today. If this is so I fear I will be deposed from my exalted possition of 2nd in command. We are off on the treck again tonight at 1.30 am.

[Monday] Oct 12 [entered as Aug 12]

We got under away at the above unpleasantly early hour and marched about 6 miles. We then were told officially - we had had our orders before – that we were being taken on in motor lorries. This I considered an excellent arrangement and after waiting about 4 hours during which we lit fires & endeavoured to keep warm, sure enough dozens of busses, lorries etc turned up. The Bn at once embussed, 22 to a bus, which did not allow for yesterday's rations. There was not room for half our company so I was left behind & came on an hour later with the 8th Bde. This was an excellent arrangement as, being an unattached officer a Frenchman gave me a lift in his car. After having tramped along these roads so long at the regulatory 3 miles an hour it was A1 to get along again at a good pace, and we seemed to be going at a breakneck speed the whole time. This idea was no doubt strengthened by my watching the speedometer & thinking the whole time it was reading miles.

We reached Sains at about midday and again billeted. All the transport had been sent on before, and had not come up yet. These were the first dirty billets we have been in. The rooms all looked as if they had not been swept for a month and their beds were filthy. The 9 officers arrived in the afternoon. Hardman & Gorst who I know and like. Moxon and .... [blank] who I know and dislike. 3 captains all apparently pleasant and two other subalterns.

We have got Sir Francis Waller and Gorst in Z coy. So I returned to the more humble possition of platoon commander. This rather upsets the mess, we were all very snug before and so at present I rather resent all these interlopers, necessary as they are from a military point of view.

On the 11th we marched all day covering nearly 18 miles of road & advancing about 10 miles. The road was very windy & also we wandered about a good deal. We expected to get into touch with the Deutcher again, but he was not forthcoming, so after waiting by a canal for sometime we returned to billets at Busnes. Here the houses were not only dirty but the people were enclined to be uncivil too & would not let us have anything more than they were absolutely obliged. We got there in the dark & the

most awful catastrophe that has happened in the whole campaign here befell me. I was wandering about in a farm yard, looking for straw etc for the men, when the ground gave way from beneath me & I sank up to my waist into a well of manure water! Fortunately, I carry clean socks, drawers etc. so I was able to change into them while my servant washed all my clothes. This misfortune appeared to me to be so serious that I was at a loss to understand what people found to laugh at until my servant, having washed my clothes went in search of some wood to make a fire to dry them, & went head over heels into it himself. In the morning my bags were still wet and on the top of all these misfortunes, 1 brace and 4 other trouser buttons came off as a result of their bath, so that I found the cold foggy morning rather apt to set up unexpected draughts.

[Wednesday] Oct 14

I started off on the 12th in my indecent trouserings and after a short march we reached Vieille Chappelle. The fifth division had come into action on our right and here we found the passage of the river barred. The Bde was in reserve, so we waited about all day on the road behind the village while the other 2 Bdes took the crossings of the river.

It was quite a change after the last few days peace to hear the Obus [type of shell] buzzing about again and I was glad to find that my little attack of "nerves" was over – not that they were very severely tested. At dusk we marched back about a mile to our billets in a farm. We have relieved the French cavalry here and they had been billeting in our farm for about a week. They seem to have taken just what they wanted & never paid for a penny worth. So when I settled up for what we had had she thought I was pulling her leg.

The next day we returned to the village & have been here ever since. It rained all yesterday & last night so we have taken up our quarters in a shop with some sheets behind it. This is not at all a bad place at all as they have an excellent cooking range and we have been having apple dumplings & jam puddings etc.

Last night my platoon was on piquet [adding fencing] on the road outside and I found 15 wounded wandering about in the rain. On enquiring I found they had been doing this for 2 hours looking for the ambulance. They were all walking cases but some had not seen a doctor at all. I got them into a shed & procured some straw & sent for our own doctor & to Bde Hd Qrs [Headquarters] for the ambulance. The doctor was in bed & said it would be much better not to touch the temporary bandages until the ambulance had got them. This man is The Gadarene Swine [St Matthew 8: 28-36].

Today still moist & muggy & still in reserve in the village. First mail for 4 days, but only one parcel from Miss Pilditch, with Comforts for the Suffering Troops. This works like another change of base.

No further diary entries were made. However, at the very back of his journal Freddy kept an updated list of all officers in his battalion and noted when any of them were wounded or killed in action including where and when. Four days later, on Sunday 18 October 1914, at the age of 24 years, Freddy was dead with nobody to add him to his list.

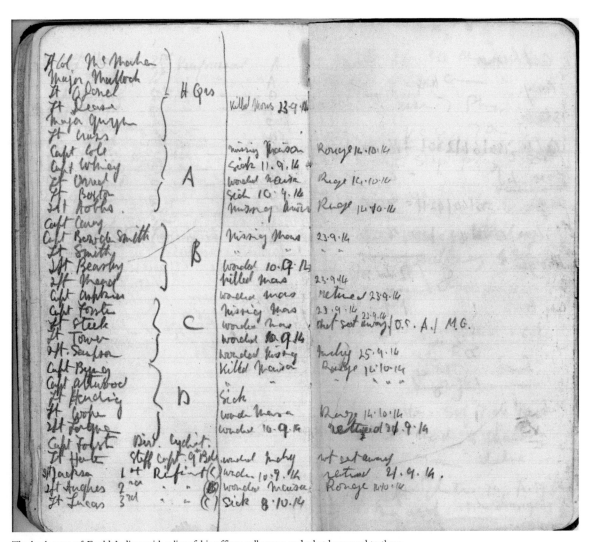

The back page of Freddy's diary with a list of his officer colleagues and what happened to them.

LETTERS FROM FREDDY

Following his death, Freddy's mother collected a range of letters sent by him to friends and family and transcribed them to ensure the family had as complete a collection as possible. Those transcripts have survived and provide a valuable insight into the life of a soldier at the beginning of the conflict that was to become the Great War. A mixture of humour and horror together with a real dose of reality are heard in this candid collection of feelings and news from the front. The Victorian formality of relationships is evident in how Freddy signs his letters, there being only one person he reserves his first name for when signing off.

Albany Barracks, Parkhurst, I[sle] of W[ight].
July 27. 1914

My dear Paw,

Things seem to be getting rather exciting. The "Precautionary Period" was declared at 4.30 this afternoon. It did not get through to us till 7, and we are all off to our forts, armed to the teeth with revolvers etc; by a train at 9 tonight. I am taking the officers' baggage and food on by car, so I have a few minutes to wait now. They will keep us in these forts until either war is declared, or things have settled down a bit.

No time for more.
Your loving son,
F. Longman

Albany Barracks, Parkhurst, I of W.
July 31 1914

My dear Paw,

... I have taken to living in darkness like Uncle Snakey. I don't go to bed till about 4.a.m. till 7.a.m. and then again at 2.p.m. till 6.p.m. Everything is very war like; recruits wandering about with loaded rifles, and every pleasure steamer from Brighton or Ryde being followed round by two great guns! We have been expecting to mobilise all today.

Best love,
Your loving son, F. Longman

Albany Barracks,
Parkhurst, I of W.
1.45 a.m.   August 2 1914

My dear Maw,

Strange to relate, I am rather enjoying all this set out. You see I am cock of my own little dung hill (no dog, I do not roll) and that is always rather fun. This is what is happening at present. 8 p.m. – 4 a.m. all my men are either on sentry, or sleeping at their posts ready to go on, and I have to go round constantly to see that they are awake and know their jobs. Then 8 a.m. – 1 p.m. they are all hard at work, making loopholes, filling sand bags and clearing away hedges, woods etc. There is an enormous amount to do (it all ought to have been done years ago, but it would never do to appear prepared!) and as the men are awake most of the night I cannot make them do more than 4 hrs work; also I have not got nearly enough tools, and may not touch off German property.

In the afternoon we all sleep in theory, in practice I am answering continuous telephone calls and arranging for feeding the men etc. So, if it goes on many months, I shall be fairly sleepy by the end of it. The post is armed with 3 six inch guns and is an "Examination Battery", i.e. any boat which comes in sight is covered by the guns, an admiralty tug then goes and examines it and if satisfactory it is allowed to pass. After sunset, any and every boat has to come and anchor in Sandown Bay. If any boat comes along without a light, the search lights find it, and it is fired on without warning. None of this is very interesting off the spot, but I am enjoying it rather. Now to beg. Could you order for me from the Stores. Have wired.

6 prs cotton drawers; 12 prs of thick unbleached socks (handmade for choice); 1 Housewife; 1 Holdall to hold brushes, shaving things, sponge etc; 1 Muffler woolly to be worn with service dress.

All to be sent to Parkhurst to await arrival. Also my shooting boots, which I believe to be at dear Upp. I cant get away from this jolly old fort to order this stuff, nor have I got a Stores List and please tell them it is urgent, as any minute might be our next

Why cant these "little gentle dear" Serbs learn to behave themselves?

Lots of love, Your loving son
F. Longman

P.S. This letter was not posted for some reason and I have run out of paper. I don't know when you will get this as no boats are running tomorrow!

I imagine we have declared war, as I have just had a message through from the mainland that we may expect an attack from small raiding parties at any time. If we have done the trick I shall return to Parkhurst tomorrow or the next day and then we may be off to the Continent at any time. This is all very bad of course but it has points too!

The powers in Europe remind me of the little gentle dear boys outside the A. & N. [Army & Navy] Stores. One nips his neighbour's leg and before you can say knife, about 10 of them are hard at it.

Lots of love
Y.L.S. [Your Loving Son]
F. Longman

Albany Barracks, Parkhurst, I. of W.
August 6 1914

My dear Maw and Paw,

Many thanks for your letters which I found on returning here. I wired for all necessary kit from the stores and elsewhere, and it has all arrived, so now I am quite equipped.

We have had a very busy week at the forts. My fort, Yaverland is just north of Sandown, on the way up to Culver Cliff. Yesterday some territorials arrived and relieved us, and I had an awful job to get them to understand what was required and how to do it. No doubt in a few days they will have settled down all right. We had to be ready to start back here at a moment's notice and in the end I got the order to catch the 10.30 train at 1045! However, we did it.

Now we are very busy mobilising; reservists, horses etc. all pouring in so that there is lots to do.

Also all these reservists have to be drilled etc at all spare moments. Of course we have no idea when or where we shall go; possibly the day after tomorrow, possibly not for 6 months or ever. Now that the bust up has come, I do hope we shall have a chance of doing something, especially while we have got this Colonel.

I don't quite know what I have got at the bank, but I have something in credit. Wouldn't it be best to leave my £250 there until this show is over?

We carry 42lbs, clothes and all; we are allowed 37lbs with us, and 100lbs at the base. Everything else I am having packed and stored in the Island. Small valuables I will send home.

Best love, Your loving son
F. Longman

To S Longman [Sister]

Albany Barracks
Parkhurst, Isle of Wight
August 6 1914

My dear Sibyl,

Yours to hand and contents duly noted. How important Braughing must feel with Wm North etc really going off to mobilize.

We are back here raking in reservists, clothing them and rubbing up their drill, etc, all day, but we have one night in peace now. It seems certain that we shall be going off to the Continong soon now, and the sooner the better.

In these modern battles, lasting several days, and with high explosive shells, etc. making a great din, the strain on the nerves is great, but actual casualties are not nearly so numerous as they used to was; probably not more than 5%.

The Garrison gunners have been having a good time. One reported a hostile air-ship which turned out to be the moon, and several guns have been going off when they least expected them.

Today, I have been packing my kit most scientifically with a weighing machine, weighing every toothbrush and sock; at present I am 39lbs and have to knock off 4 and I am blowed if I know what to sacrifice.

Lots of love,
Your loving brother
F. Longman

Albany Barracks, Parkhurst, I of W
August 9 1914.

My dear Maw,

Here we are still, and with no orders to go. We are completely mobilized now and could be on the march in half an hour. I have got my 35 lbs packed to a ¼ of a pound. As far as I can see we shall not be allowed to write many letters or even keep a diary for fear of news leaking out; so all I shall be able to send probably will be an official P.C. with various sentences printed and the untrue ones crossed off.

Our address will be;
4th Bn. Royal Fusiliers
9th Infantry Brigade
3rd Division
2nd Army Corps
British Expeditionary Force

The RGA [Royal Garrison Artillery] in one of our forts here reported a hostile airship the other day; it turned out to be the moon. Another one fired on one of the Examination boats and said that a wireless message let the gun off! All this is most satisfactory. I have just heard a strong rumour that we leave Southampton on Monday night, but this is "strictly confidential". We have a pretty good idea of where we are going and roughly what we shall have to do, but I must not say in case the letter went astray.

I hope we shall pass through a good number of countries as I am told each one will probably stump up with a medal, which would make one feel fearfully important. It really is lucky that since we have to scrap, the Colonel is still in command as everyone has such confidence in him.

How you can have the face to muzzle that dog while the G.E. [German Enemy] can show his face, I can't think.

Best love,
Y.L.S.
F. Longman

(Letter to Mr Pilditch) [Philip Pilditch]

Yaverland Fort
Sandown
I. of W.
3 a.m. August 11 1914

My dear Old Pills

As far as I can see I shall be going for a little jaunt on the Continong about when you are going only I shall be shooting Serbs most of the time, or will it be Montenegrons? I hate the prospect of all this military activity! When the time comes I shall probably make a bolt for Venezuela. Meanwhile, I am in command of a ruddy fort full of Toots "gambadiers". And as this means I get about 5 hours sleep a day on boards and very dull grub poor old Meeroy has been cursed very bitterly. I already owe you a letter re yeomanry. Take my advice and remain a strict civilian. The only bright spots on an otherwise blighted life are when I pull up a rediculous mediaeval drawbridge at sunset, and when I sally forth on my rounds like Brondo Bill [probably Bronco Bill] armed to the teeth with swords and a loaded revolver.

I enclose a poem which you may know. If you don't I know there are days when you would love to repeat it.

Ys. Ays. [Yours Always]
F. Longman

Albany Barracks, Parkhurst, I of W.
August 12 1914.

My dear Paw,

It is rumoured that we are off in a few hours. This is doubtful, but I must finish off all last packing in case.

I believe I have paid all my debts, large and small, and as I have been going rather a bust lately, with my kit etc, I expect I have made a fairly large hole in the £250. But my expenses from now on will be nil and there will be a fairly fat cheque for service pay, so I think I had better leave the £250 in the bank and invest it when it is all over. The Germans seem to be having a bad time at present; it looks as if it would not be a very long campaign.

Now I must rush off.

My best love to Maw, Paw and everyone

Your loving son
F. Longman

Royal Fusiliers
Parkhurst
I. of W.
August 12 - 1914

My dear Uncle Snakey,

We seem to be in for a war which must be making Old Boney, [Napoleon] wherever he may be, green with envy. And as far as one can see we are on the winning side.

The Russians will be making themselves felt in about 10 days from now and if the Germans are to do anything, they must crush France, Belgium and ourselves before then. This seems to be rather a big order, especially as the French are so thoroughly fortified.

Modern fighting seems to be rather an unpleasant affair, but attacking forts with their barbed wire and guns must be a most depressing business. I am not a blood thirsty cove by nature, but it really is a great opportunity and will be an experience which I shall be able to bore my friends and relations about for years to come.

We have heard semi-officially that we are off tomorrow, but everything is so secret that we don't know for certain. I do wish we could get a move on. I wonder if it will be all over before you leave Upp [Hall]!

I suppose it is quite on the cards that it might be. If so, I hope I may see you then.

Yr. affect nephew
F. Longman

Parkhurst
August 13 1914

My dear Maw

Off at last! We leave here at 11 and I believe go off from Southampton today.

I enclose a list of my stuff which is being stored here. I am telling them to send you a receipt for it.

1. Bureau	1. cardboard hat box
2. Deal Cases	2. canvas bags
1. Uniform case	2. tin hat boxes
1. Fishing rod	1. Chair
2. Leather Portmanteaus	1. auto wheel
1. carpet hold-all	

Everything is packed and ready and I have got my Kit that I carry on my back arranged perfectly now; all sorts of little private tweaks!

No time for more as we are just parading.
Lots of love to Maw and Paw and everyone
Y.L.S.
F. Longman

Letter to Mr Meyrick Jones

Parkhurst, I. of W.
August 13 1914

Dear Mr Meyrick

We are off to the War in about an hour's time, so as we have a few minutes to spare I thought I must write you a line before we go.

This war is a horrid business but of course it is

the opportunity that the likes of us have been waiting for. It will not be pleasant, but at any rate one will feel that one is of some use at last, which is more than one can say in peace time.

No time for more at present.

Yours ever
F. Longman

August 19 1914 (received Aug 25th)

My dear Mother,

The censor is v. strict, so I fear I can give no news except that I am exceedingly flourishing. I enclose particulars of a strange bat I caught. I hope to be able to recognise it from Millar's when I return. If you could send a pair of "Puttee stockings" they would be v. acceptable. Your first letter has arrived today.

Y.L.S.
F. Longman

Particulars of bat enclosed.

August 31. 1914 (received Sept 17th)

My dear mother and father,

I fear it is a long time since I have written, but for the last 8 days or so letters have been impossible.

I can now give you some news up to a week ago, though I expect you have seen it all in the paper by now. We landed at Havre and camped about 8 miles out at Harfleur. The march out was rather disastrous, the hottest day I have ever known and the men very tired from the crossing and the disembarking, also still soft; before we got to camp over 200 had fallen out. However, we were by no means the worst, and they soon got hard again. There we stayed 2 days while it rained harder than I thought possible the whole time. The whole place was a "stinking muck heap" at once, and the men and all our kit soaked.

Then we trained via Rouen to Landrecies and went into billets at a place called Noyelle. Here we stayed 4 days and had a most peaceful time. A very nice place with plenty of excellent grub, nice people and a river to bathe in. From there we went by two good marches to Mons, where we had our first scrap. We were ordered to hold a line of canal and to delay the enemy as long as possible; we barricaded bridges, dug trenches etc. We had left our last halting place at 3 a.m., Saturday 22nd and were ready for action early Sunday morning, working all night with no sleep. About 10 a.m. the show began and lasted most of the day. My company did not come under rifle fire but had plenty of shrapnel. I had one little excitement; there were some big barges on the canal which had to be burnt, 2 of them did not catch, so I had to set them going. When I got there I found that 2 or 3 snipers had got the range of it, so that with an occasional shell bursting, I did not waste much time. Only two of our companies were closely engaged, and they lost 150 men, killed and wounded, 5 officers killed and 2 wounded, 1 slightly. Poor Jo Mead was killed also Fred Forster.

This is very sketchy, but I am trying to keep a diary and there is not much time. Fred Sampson has since been wounded rather severely and had to be left behind in a school to the Germans who blew up the place: I only hope someone could remove him first. I can tell you nothing about this week, but we are all going strong.

Very few letters have got through to us. I have had mother's first, one from father dated 18th, and one from Aunt Mary dated 21st.

Could you send me two silk handkerchiefs as near khaki colour as possible.

The war is rather a beastly business, the peasants get such a bad time. I do hate seeing the poor things turning out of their homes and legging it along the roads goodness knows where, but we are all very flourishing ourselves. Best love to everybody.

Your loving son
F.L.

Official P. C. Arrived same day, Sept 19th [as letter dated 19th Sept]

I am quite well
I have received your letter
Letter follows first opportunity

F. Longman

September 1 1914

September 3 1914

My dear mother and father,

I have been carrying enclosed letter about some time but cannot post it yet. Meanwhile, I have had letters 1. 2. 3. 5. 6, and was <u>very</u> pleased to get them. Being an undutiful son I fear I laughed at Paw's misfortunes (*he tumbled into the pond H.A.L.*). [Harriet Ann Longman] I hope I shall see Ambrose over here some time. No doubt you will know more about the general situation than we do, but the Russians seem to be coming it "rayther powerful".

The following are my wants, though none of them are important.

Newspapers
2 khaki silk hanks
A light waterproof bag containing boracic powder
40 frcs French money if possible
Caramels (Willy's brand)!

I am thoroughly enjoying my walking tour on the Continong just at present. I wonder when the next scrap will be.

Y.L.S. F.L.

Sept 5 1914

Still going strong and I believe the post goes today. The other news a week old is, another scrap on Monday 24th, 30 miles march on 25th -, another scrap on 26th -, details later.

Another want is a scrapping map of Europe, on canvas.

Best love. F.L.

**On active service
September 8 1914**

My dear Mother and Father,

Thanks for your letter and enclosure. I will take the pink – or is it fizzy – daily as directed. I don't think there was much amiss; we were all rather weary after the retreat, and I expect I was a little run down, but since then I have been exceptionally flourishing. I have been employed as Railway Transport Officer for two days, but I have now rejoined the Regiment thank goodness. We missed our express Post Card day, but hope to get another on the 10th. Meanwhile, I am sending a long list of wants, in case our second P.C. fails. Curiously enough, I have been wearing a tummie [?] belt for some time, and as I always wrap my woolly scarf round that well developed member when sleeping out, I feel that I must deserve to be "up" with Aunt Mary.

Here are my wants.
A pair of strong fur lined gloves.
A pair of shooting mittens.
2 pairs of thick woolly vests and 2 pairs of thick woolly short pants.
2 khaki coloured hunting stocks, size 15½ and 2 do 16½ (for O'Donel) with 12 cheap gold pins for do. I believe Drew of Piccadilly, next door to Spink, has these or can get them.
1 pair thick greased marching boots with iron tips and heels and "domes of silence" sort of nails. Maxwells of Dover Street have my measurements. And so I suppose they had better make the boots although they are thieves. Please tell them to make them on the large side, as I can always wear 2 prs of socks if they are too big: and lastly a knife: it should if possible have the following in it: a large blade for table use, a tin opener and corkscrew, also a chain and attachment for braces button. This is a long list and none of the things are immediately necessary, but as the nights get colder they will become very welcome, especially if we have another spell in the trenches.

Just at present we are some way from the front, but no doubt we shall soon be at it again. I fear it does not look as if I was going to slay many pheasants this season unless I can snare one here. I must purchase some raisins!

Yesterday I got at a grocer who had not been ransacked by the troops and was able to make up a basket for the mess. My french managed all right, but it quite broke down at pumice stone, all I could get was a bicycle pump and a gas bracket!

While I have been out here I have been in all the churches I have had the chance to, but although the buildings are very fine, generally inside they are spoilt to my mind by the highly coloured images etc, and old monuments seem to be very scarce; talking of which, the modern French cemetery ornament is enough to make a dog sick!

No more news at present, all our movements are "wrap" in mystery and we know rather less about them than anyone else.

Your loving son
F. Longman

September 11 1914
(Received Sept. 19.)

My dear mother

Just a line to say I am "OK", in case I am reported wounded, which I think is most unlikely. All I have got is a clean small pellet hole through the fleshy part of my right arm, which did not touch any bones, arteries etc. As usual I had the luck of the old un; one pellet went through my puttees, one through my left sleeve, one through my revolver bolster and a ricochet through my Burberry all down my right side, none of which touched a hair. My news will have to wait to get a bit staler before I can let you have it. The last letter I got was dated 27th since when we have had no mails. I have thought of one more want, a sheet of waterproof stuff, like your sponge bag to tie my bread and cheese ration up in, for my haversack. Best love to everybody. Y.L.S.
F. Longman

Official P. C. Arrived Sept 20th
September 12

I am quite well
I have been admitted into hospital and am going on well
V.S. [Very Slightly] wounded and hope to be discharged soon.
I am being sent down to the rail head.
Letter follows first opportunity

F. Longman

POST OFFICE TELEGRAPHS
[FROM WAR OFFICE]
15th September 1914

To C.J. Longman Esq Upp Hall Braughing Herts

Regret to inform you that 2nd Lieut. F. Longman Royal Fusiliers is reported missing.

From Secretary, War Office

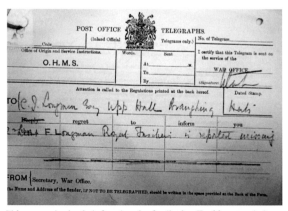

Telegram mistakenly informing the family that Freddy was missing in action

Letter to Mr Pilditch and Mr Alison

September 17 1914

Dear Pills and Feet,

Just a line to say that all is well, and to pour out my woes to you as of yore. We started off at Mons, beginning at 3 a.m. Saturday morning. We had 3 scraps and marched nearly 100 miles in 5 days with only 8 hours sleep. Since then we have been in touch with these blasted Germans nearly every day. Altogether we have had 6 officers almost certainly killed, 7 men or less – chiefly less – seriously wounded and 3 sick, so we have not many left. Now we are advancing again thank goodness and raking in a few Germans, anything from 20 - 50 every day. A week ago we bagged 1500 at one go. That day I got it rather hot. I had to reinforce a firing line under machine gun fire at 400+ [yards] and when we got there we were lying on the skyline pooping at Germans in a wood. I lost 10 men from the remains of my little platoon and got one pellet through the puttee, one through the left sleeve, one through my revolver holster, a ricochette which ripped open the side of my Burbery and finally a clean little hole through the fleshy part of my right arm which did not touch the bone, or an artery or anything! Did you ever hear of such luck? They sent me down to the advanced base fort, and today I was reported fit to return to duty, thank goodness.

So much for my troubles. Meanwhile, we are all very cheerful and I manage to find a good deal of amusement in the intervals. But Pills these shells do put the fear of God into me, though actually they do very little damage indeed.

Toot is in our Division, and I see him fairly often. He was wounded slightly in the arm and hand at Mons and also had his horse shot under him. He then got mixed up with another Division for a week but has returned to us again now. Joe Mead and Fred Sampson who I think you know are both dead. This leaves me rather forlorn as they were the two fellows I knew and liked best in the Regt. But it all comes in the day's work and Joe did awfully well. He was hit in the head quite early in the day at Mons, but he stuck to it under a damnable fire until he got another right through the forehead. This is a most depressing letter

to send you, especially as at present I am anything but depressed. We hear reports of Canadian, Indian, Australian, New Zealand, S. African, Japanese, Russian and Montenegrin reinforcements coming in on all sides and I feel absolutely sure that we shall hammer these fellows within two months.

I am combining this letter between you two as every letter has to be censored and they hate us if we produce long epistles like this very often. I send it you first Pills as I know your address and have forgotten Feets. If he does not get it I dare say he will get over the disappointment. So farewell you two old ghosts. My, what a dinner we shall have when I return!

Yrs ever F. Longman

September 17 1914
(Received Sept 22nd)

My dear mother

Here I am in civilisation again, - where it does not matter at present. I was sent sick with my arm for 2 days, and from that I have been shifted from place to place till at last I have fetched up at the advanced base, just as my woundlet healed. Today I have been passed fit to rejoin, and I may get orders to entrain in 10 minutes, or 3 days, according as to how the trains fit in. I have done a record amount of grousing at each and all of the R.A.M.C. [Royal Army Medical Corps] coves [blokes] I have come across, for fussing and mucking about my arm. But for all that it is very nice to get a **Bath** and clean clothes again, and decent meals off clean table cloths; if only it were not for the fact that our fellows are scrapping every day and I ought to be there. If they have a big show, as seems probable and I miss it, I shall be very sick.

Meanwhile, I left the day before the first mail we have had for 12 days came in and I hear there were several letters and parcels for me. I hope they will keep them. I have been laying in all sorts of tinned meats, milk, chocolate etc etc, which will be very welcome to the mess when I return.

The scrap when I got hit is now a week old, so I can give a few more details. I really saw very little of the scrap in general, but what happened in my little corner was this. We were vanguard to the Bde [Brigade] and coming round a corner we saw about three miles of German transport winding along a road on the opposite side of a valley about two miles ahead. We chased after it at once and the company in front of ours came into action on the side of a hill, firing into a wood at the foot at 400 x [yards]. They came under a very heavy fire from a machine gun and rifles and after a bit I had to reinforce with my platoon. We had about 100 yds. to double in the open and as soon as we showed of course they turned the whole of their fire on us. The ground seemed to be alive with pellets all round, and my wig how I ran! Only 3 men were hit, none seriously, and I got a pellet through my puttee. Once in the firing line it was not so bad, as we could keep their fire down with our own, and we soon had the machine gun out of action. (Three other people claim to have done this, but I still put in my little claim). I got hold of a rifle here and had 150 steady aimed shots at heads at 400 yds, so I 'ave 'opes. While we were here I had two of my little platoon killed and three more wounded and got 3 more pellets through my clothes. Just before they surrendered I got the pellet in the arm, but with my usual luck it touched nothing, and hurt very little. We captured 1500 Germans that day, 2 machine guns and a good deal of baggage.

This is the hottest corner I am every likely to be in, so now that is over the sooner I get back the better.

I am sending you my diary up to date from here. I doubt if you can read any of it as it was written in all sorts of places, and with the idea of being copied. Also it is rather disjointed and mixed. When I return I will piece it all together and copy it out if I can read it myself. Meanwhile, when it arrives, which will not be for a week or a fortnight, if you can decipher any of it, there it is.

I wonder if all this will pass the censor! I think it ought to. Best love to all

Your loving son
F. Longman

(Letter to H.G. Comber Esq. Pembroke College)

September 17 1914

My dear Old Man

Just a line to say I am going strong and have seen Toot who is very fit. Any news I could give you that would be of interest is forbidden by the censor. So all I can talk about is my own little part of the show. We started at Mons with the most strenuous time I have ever had. In five days we had three scraps, in each case preparing a position i.e. digging etc; marched over 80 miles and had 8 hours sleep. Toot was slightly wounded the first day in the arm and again in the hand; also he had his horse shot under him. He then got mixed up with another Division for a week and returned to us about a fortnight ago. Since then we have been in touch with the enemy practically every day, our Brigade being taken for rear guard or advanced guard incessantly. A week ago we had a most pronounced success, when we took 1500 prisoners, some machine guns and a lot of baggage. I had a very hot corner there. I had to reinforce a firing line on a sky line under machine gun fire at 400+ [yards]. I lost 10 men killed and wounded from the remains of my little platoon and had four pellets through my clothes and one through the fleshy part of my arm. A very slight wound which just missed the bone and was passed fit today. However, I had to go down to the advanced base from where I am writing. I should dearly love to toast my backside in front of your fire again, Old Man and hear just how soon these Germans will be hammered and see Fred wax indignant over it all.

I don't think the censor can complain of anything I have said but if I continue much longer he will tear it up in disgust. Altogether we have lost six officers killed including Fred Sampson I fear, seven wounded and three sick.

Yrs. v. sincerely
F Longman

(Letter to Susan Minet, Hadham Hall)

September 18 1914
(received Sept. 24th)

My dear Susan,

As I am censor at present, I am taking the opportunity to send a shower of letters to all deserving people. Mother gets all the official news from me. And as I have just sent a large budget to her, I will trust to your being able to get it out of her.

At present I am staying in a hotel at our advanced base, a fairly large town in S.W. France. I had a slight wound in the arm, not enough really to stop my doing things, but as all the ambulances, hospitals, etc. at the front are packed, they sent me down here. Now I am hourly expecting orders to rejoin my regiment, and meanwhile am being employed at various odd jobs; today it is censoring. It is rather annoying kicking ones heels here, when I know all the time our people are hard at it, at the front. If the show goes on much longer I shall be to talk French! At present I have no difficulty in getting whatever I want, and I can understand a good deal of general conversation but cant take part in it. My dinner hour is up now and I must return to censor more letters.

Please thank Aunt Mary for her letter, and tell Geoff if he does not write soon, I will scrag him when I return

Yr affect. 1st. cousin
F. Longman

(Letter to S Longman)

September 18 1914

My dear Sibyl,

As I am the censor myself today, I am sending off letters to all and sundry. It is thus how. As you have heard or will know from my letter and diary to mother, I have had a slight pellet in the arm. This is now passed fit, and I have been "returned to duty". So until they can get me back to the front again I am

doing work in an office, and the job they have turned me onto is censoring letters. There are hundreds of thousands of them, some ten days old and nearly all worse written even than mine! Some are exceedingly amusing, and most follow the same lines. They all begin, "Hoping this will find you as it leaves me. A.I." One letter by the time I had done with it read,

"Dear Sal,
all's well,
Alf"

I got a letter of yours about a fortnight ago, since then there had not been a mail. I am glad the Boomer is up. I see Toot fairly often, as he is in our Division. He got a slight wound in the arm and hand and had a horse shot under him at Mons, otherwise he is v. fit. Will this show affect New Zealand? Maybe it will be over by then, I hope so. I don't expect I shall see Brose as he is in a different army, but I should love to see him hobnobbing with the furriner.

I am not going to repeat news, and if you can't read my diary you will have to wait till I return. I wonder if I shall summon up energy to copy the thing out!

Best love,
Your loving brother
F. Longman

[Letter from Charles Longman, Freddy's father, to HM War Office)

September 18 1914

The Manager
Engineers Dept
H.M. War Office.

Dear Sir,

I should be exceedingly grateful for any news respecting my son, 2nd Lieutenant F. Longman, 4th Battn Royal Fusiliers. He was reported to be "missing" by telegram to me on Sept. 15th, but appeared, to my relief, in the list of Sept 17th as wounded. On enquiry at the War Office it appeared the wrong telegram had been sent. I hope to hear soon where he is, the nature of the wound and how he is progressing.

I am, your obedient servant
C.J. Longman

September 22 1914 (Received October 2nd)

My dear Mother,

I am back with the Regiment, thank goodness; though I find we have lost an awful lot of officers and men in my absence. Byng and Attwood of my Company are both killed. I am sorry about Byng, I have been in his company since I joined, and he has always been exceedingly nice; helping in unobtrusive ways, and trying to look fierce all the time. Also Cole and Hobbs killed, Orred and Hughes wounded. This brings our total up to nine almost certainly killed, nine wounded (counting me as wounded) and three sick. I knew I should miss the really big show. They had a really big show on last Saturday week, and then for eight days they have been in trenches, constantly under fire from guns, machine guns and rifles. They were counter attacked time after time, by day and night; and the whole time they did not budge an inch. Now they have been relieved by the 6th Division and we are billeted about six miles back in reserve to the Army.

I had hoped to find a whole budget of letters waiting for me, and I did find no. 10 from you and one from Sibyl, with your socks, handkerchiefs, ointment and pencil enclosed, all of which will be most useful. But sad to relate they had sent all my letters after me and I missed them on the road, so no man can tell when I shall get them again, if ever, the puttees I got before I left.

We are now only two miles from the place where I was in hospital two days, before going up to the advanced base. I came back here with a train load of stragglers, who had been rounded up and sent down to the base to reorganise. There were about 800 of them, and they were a lot of beauties! When we got here, I delivered those who belonged to the 8th Brigade to their owners, who were up in the firing line, and a jolly time I had, as it had to be done after

dark: only two Scotchmen escaped me.

I was rather amused to see in a paper that an officer in the Guards was patted on the back very much for having carried a wounded brother officer out of the firing line under heavy fire; the same day three of our fellows were sentenced to 14 days field imprisonment by the Colonel for doing exactly the same thing! And of course the Colonel was perfectly right or else every wounded man would have six gentlemen with cold feet carrying him away. Our 35lb kits have come up, and I have been through Joe Meades to see if there are any papers, etc. to send to his people. I am not looking forward to writing to them, but I expect they would like to hear anything I can tell about him.

I saw in a fairly recent Times I got at the base that Feet is engaged to be married to Miss Prest. Prest was at Pembroke, and her father is very rich and a director of Eley Bros. So Feet has done well! I knew it was in the wind some time ago and am awfully glad to hear of it. I expect he is very busy cartridge making!

Well done Jack! (our groom HAL)) It is good to hear of everybody turning out so splendidly at home. I hope some of the Braughing section will think better of it and volunteer for foreign service. If they want to enlist they should go to Hounslow and join the Fusiliers and we will give them plenty to do. When John (our footman HAL) is fit again he must come along as I am in need of a servant. Best love to all,

Your loving son, F. Longman

Later, same day.

I have just got your and Sibyl's letters dated 9th & 11th with the enclosures, for which ever so many thanks. The boracic powder in socks game is most effective, and as the lid came off, it was already done for me. Also a large packet of home knitted socks which I will distribute to the platoon, and which are the best things I can give them. Please thank all knitters for them. Also a letter from Susan, dated Sept 10, in which she says Ambrose had grown a flowing beard. I bet mine beat it, mine would have put the average goat to confusion. I am now consoled for missing my other letters, and well set up for socks, hankies. etc.

Best love.
Y.L.S.
F. Longman

P.S. I don't know Miss Prest but I fear she may be a little smart; Feet likes 'em so! Please tell Sibyl I wrote to the little rotundity (Pills, not Nan) a few days ago.

**September 24 1914
(Received Oct 3 with previous letter)**

My dear mum

As we are still resting after our exertions, either in trenches or at the Advanced Base, I may as well write while there is some chance of a post going out.

At present we are in very comfortable billets, with plenty of grub, and a post in and out every day. Today I got a letter from Sibyl with an enclosure from you dated Aug 14th! Both very welcome. It is getting rather cold at nights now, and though at present I have had nothing to grouse about, it makes one realise that campaigning in the winter here will be most unpleasant; so I have designed a winter kit and I wonder if you, or perhaps it would be easier for the Fox, [Freddy's older brother William] would order it for me from Dege of 13 Conduit Street. He has my measurements as he made my hunting kit and some breeches since.

The coat I want to be made of enclosed stuff and lined with thick Jaeger [wool]. If they could do anything in the way of double cuffs, so that the inside (Jaeger) one could turn down it would be a good plan. Also I want the collar to be fairly deep, so as to turn up round my neck. The whole coat should be roomy to allow for thick under-wear. If my second star has appeared in the Gazette they can put it on. All pockets as big as possible, and right bottom one lined with leather to carry cartridges. Buttons tarnished as much as possible.

The knickerbockers I want made of thick corduroy (most irregular, but these things do not matter now-a-days!) and rather baggy at the knees

with four buttons below the knees and then thin extensions to half way down my calf. I could write straight to Dege but they will be so scandalised that they will be sure to say it is all impossible at first, especially the double cuff. But I have no doubt they will do it, if whoever explains is firm. There is no immediate hurry, but a night I had out the other day made me realise that it will be most unpleasant in six weeks.

An aeroplane has just dropped a bomb into our village, doing no harm to anyone, though it made a roof look foolish. It was not meant for us, but for another aeroplane below it. I travelled up with James Gammell the other day, which was very cheerful. Three more Sp. [Special] Reserve Officers have arrived, one who I was at Pembroke with and dislike very cordially.
Best love,
Your loving son,
F. Longman

(Two official printed postcards sent on September 25 1914 and both received 6.11.14)

<u>1st Postcard</u>

~~I am quite well~~
~~I have been admitted into hospital~~
~~sick/wounded~~
~~and I am going on well~~
~~and I hope to be discharged soon~~
~~I am being sent down to the base~~
~~I have received your letter/telegram/parcel~~
Letter follows at first opportunity
~~I have received no letter from you~~
~~lately/for a long time~~

Signature only: F. Longman
Date: 25.9.14

<u>2nd Postcard</u> All erased but the following,

I am quite well
I have received your letter/parcel
Letter follows at first opportunity

F. Longman 25.9.14

(Letter to Mary Minet)

September 25 1914 (Hadham Hall Oct 5. 14)

My dear Aunt Mary,

Many thanks for your P.C. which I got today. I am glad Geoff is getting some partridges this year, I only hope he will leave a few for next. I have been indulging in a long rest, first because of my arm, and now with the Regiment. Whilst I was away the Battalion has been distinguishing itself greatly, and French, Smith Dorrien (C.O.C. Army), [General Officer Commanding-in-Chief] Hamilton G.O.C. Division [General Officer Commanding] and Shaw (G.O.C. Brigade) have all been over, and personally congratulated them. So we are all in a high state of delight!

I wish I had seen Brose's Zeppelin come down; though if you are writing to him, you might tell him that we fetched down an aeroplane all on our own. This was the incident I have enjoyed most. Today we are returning to the trenches, so I don't suppose I shall write again for some time.

Your loving nephew
F. Longman

September 27 1914
(Received Oct 3rd)

My dear Maw,

I have just got your letter of the 18th and am very indignant with the muddle headed old War Office. There can be absolutely no excuse for them to report me missing, as my wound was so slight that I did not report sick till we got in that evening, and did not leave the Regiment till next day; and the casualty list had been sent in before I went. It is too bad of them to make these mistakes, and I believe they are always doing it.

I am glad letters have begun to arrive; now that the retreat is over, a post goes out daily, and they ought to be coming in regularly. I sent off an official postcard as soon as I knew I was reported wounded, and these are supposed to go straight through, so I hope you got news soon after writing your letter. Meanwhile, here we are in the trenches again. I have got a very snug little cubby hole, dug out of the side of a bank. This morning I spent in fitting it with all modern conveniences, such as steps down, a cupboard, niches for a mug, plates etc; and sundry bits of packing case to prevent land slips. The German is a methodical bird and seems to shell us at stated times, and generally in the same places, so all is very pleasant and serene, and with the help of Pickwick [by Charles Dickens] and much food, I am prepared to remain here until the French and Russians have finished off the war. I fear they will have to battle a bit, as I propose being home for the November shoot.

Just behind my bomb proof shelter is a poplar tree about the size of the one on the left of the ball gates [at Upp Hall]. A German high explosive hit it about 15ft from the ground and cut if off quite as clean as if I had done it with an axe and nearly as clean as if old Palmer had [gardener and gamekeeper at Upp Hall]. A small bit of the shell dropped onto the floor of my hole, and I have pocketed it. I was very pleased to get cousin May's letter and will answer it one of these days, also one from Tick today. I got the one she sent to Parkhurst. I am beginning to loathe these old Whistling Rufuses [Shells from a gun named after a popular marching song, Whistling Rufus]. One never quite knows when and where they will burst, and if they burst on top of us they make such a din. The French seem to be having a great set to miles away on our left.

I always seem to be thinking of fresh wants; today it is condensed milk and tinned butter periodically. I sent an experimental Official P.C. off yesterday with "Tin condensed milk" on it, I wonder if it was passed, and if it went through any quicker. "Roll on the end of the War", as the men always end their letters.

Your loving son
F. Longman

P.S. What is Foxe's date? 25 Oct? (*for going to India HAL*)

[Fox is a nickname for William, Freddy's brother]

(Letter to Mr Meyrick Jones)

On Active Service
October 1 1914

Dear Mr Meyrick,

Thanks so much for your letter which I was delighted to get. This woundlet of mine – it might be called "yoar", for is it not a little one? – has been a great piece of luck for me. For in the first place I got a week's holiday including a bath and clean underclothes, out of it; and secondly all my friends and relations have been writing to condole, and the arrival of a letter is a great event. No, I have not been neglecting to take cover; for one thing I dursn't and for another I think it is just as bad for an officer to expose himself unnecessarily as it is for a man to bolt. We have lost a great many too many officers through this sort of "Tom Fool" pluck. When I copped it, it was like this. I had to reinforce another company of ours on the side of a hill. The enemy were at the bottom and the only cover to be had was a little pathway which of course put us on the skyline, so really we would have had a very bad time if the Deutcher was not such a rotten bad shot. We had a very strenuous time to start with – Starting from the Saturday before Mons, we had three scraps marched roughly 80 miles, entrenched three positions in five days, with only eight hours sleep. Then we did the retreat, long marches and constantly in touch with our friends the Enemy. This was rather trying and for the first time in five years I really had the mastery over my waist measurements (it is as bad as ever now). When we advanced again all was well, and all the men wanted to get some of their own back. The men have been A.1., always cheerful and willing, and splendid when under fire, though of course there are a few black sheep. The only disappointments are the Scotch. They cannot march and do not seem to care much about fighting. There are three Scotch Rgts in our Division, and they are easily the worst three.

Of course I cant tell you any recent news, but I dont think there is any harm in saying that we are snugly entrenched in a very extensive position, with plenty of grub. And letters regularly, and only a reasonable proportion of shells and snipers just to keep our eyes in, perhaps there might be a little more sleep. We started with 25 officers, and have been reinforced by five; of these nine have almost certainly been killed, 11 wounded, and three returned home sick, so you see we leave not many left unscathed.

Now I have talked enough about myself! I was delighted to get the photograph of Mrs Meyrick and the kin. The stuff is all there, a little hardening of the muscles perhaps and he will be the as "likelyest" fly weight I have seen. It is good to hear how splendidly people are turning out at home. Kaiser Bill must be rather sorry he tried to take this hornet's nest. I only hope it will be over in time to shoot an old cock or two before next season. The only annoying part about my arm was that the W.O. [War Office] reported me "missing" at home, and gave them a bad 36 hrs, before they changed to "wounded". Too bad of 'im! The weather is perfect; the mornings have a nip in them, just the sort of days when you would have hounded Arthur Pawson and others away from the library fire after breakfast! This is a long and weary epistle I fear, but you have some practice in reading my hieroglyphics.

Love to all
Yours affect'ly
F. Longman

On active service
October 2 1914

Dear Mr Mead,

By the time you receive this letter, you will of course have had the sad news of your son. But as I have always looked on Joe as my best friend since we have been in the Regiment together, I thought you might like to hear what little news I can give of him.

From the time we landed he was all eagerness to get to work; sparing no pains in preparing his platoon and getting to know all his men personally.

He was always cheerful, and if any of his contemporaries were depressed, we only had to go to Joe to be cheered up.

We had many a long chat together in the evenings on the way to Mons, and I have often heard him say that if it was his fate to be hit, his only regret would be the sorrow it would cause at home.

When we got to Mons his company was in reserve to Capt. Ashburner's, which was defending the bridge over the canal. It was a hopeless position as the enemy could get up to within 100 yds of the bridge and then fire from houses, gardens, etc and never be seen. Also I believe five different Battalions were recognized in front of this one company. Joe was soon ordered to reinforce the firing line, which he did in the face of a fearful fire. As he was doing this he was hit in the head, a wound that would have sent nine out of ten people to the rear to be dressed, not so Joe: he was up again in an instant and with his platoon in the trench. It was here, as he was searching for the enemies' firing line with his glasses, that he received the fatal shot in the head. It must be some consolation to you to know that no one could possibly have died more gallantly than Joe, and I know he would ask for nothing better.

It only remains for me to offer you our most heartfelt sympathy in your loss, and remain,
Yours sincerely
F. Longman

[N.B. Lieutenant Joseph Frederick Mead was killed on 23rd August 1914 aged 22].

(Letter to Mr Sampson)

On Active Service
October 2 1914

Dear Mr. Sampson

I was very surprised to hear from my people that no mention of your son had been in the paper so I hasten to write to tell you all I know about him in case you have not heard.

On August 22nd at Cambrai he was wounded in the abdomen by a shrapnel bullet, but the M.O. [Medical Officer] who examined him on the spot thought that it was not a serious wound, in fact he had hopes that it was little more than a flesh wound, though of course it is hard to tell. We had to retire

very suddenly and quickly that day and Fred had to be left behind. He was put in a temporary hospital however, with a lot more wounded and was made as comfortable as possible. In all cases that we have heard of the Germans are treating our wounded very well. So there is every reason for you to be able to hope that all is well with him.

It must be a very trying time for you all to be in suspense so long, but I feel sure he is safe enough somewhere by now. If you do get any news of him, it would be a great kindness if you would let me know, as we are all most anxious to hear from him –

Yours sincerely
F. Longman

[N.B. 2nd Lieutenant Frederick Arthur Sampson was taken prisoner of war and survived].

(Letter written to Hugo Lambert in East Africa)

On Active Service
October 2 1914

My dear Hugo,

It is ages since I have either written to, or heard from you, wherefor both of us are to be cursed. Well, here we are at this war which Scharlich promised us so confidently for the beginning of next year, – not a bad shot for him –

My battalion have been out here since the start, and were at Mons, Le Guernay and Cambrai. Then we did the retreat back to Cha[r]tre, and then back again, fighting five days on the Marne, and now nearly three weeks on the Aisne. So you see we have done our share. Poor old Joe Mead was killed the first day at Mons, and Fred Sampson was badly wounded two days later at Cambrai and had to be left behind with the Germans; altogether we have had nine officers killed, 11 wounded and three sick. I had the luck of the devil one of the days round Marne. I had to reinforce a firing line on the sky-line, under machine gun and rifle fire. My little platoon - only 25 left out of 58 - lost two killed and eight wounded. And I had a pellet through my puttees and through my left sleeve, another through my revolver holster, a ricochet which ripped all the way down the side of my coat, and finally a clean little hole through the fleshy part of my arm, which only kept me away 10 days. Did you ever hear such luck? -

I wonder if you will get the chance to have a tiff at them in W. Africa? Toot (*Walter Stuart Wingate Gray*) is out here and was slightly wounded in the arm at Mons. James [Gammell] came up in the same train as I did when I returned from being sick. He was a first reinforcement. McDougal (*Pembroke College*) is out here too and relieves us in our trenches tonight. Pills (*Philip Pilditch*) has joined some territorial gunners and hopes to come out. Feet (*cousin*) has been so busy and prosperous making cartridges for us all, that he can afford to get engaged to a Miss Prest, sister of Pembroke Prest and daughter of his boss!

The more that happens, the longer we wait, the more prodigious is the dinner we have in town when next we forgather. Hugo, it makes me feel quite faint to think of it. I am trying to send you a brain wave to answer this letter at once, as otherwise it takes such years to get out and back.

Yours ever
F. Longman

(Letter to Louisa Ricket)

On Active Service
October 2 1914

My dear Loo,

Many thanks for your letter which I was delighted to get. I am sorry I would not oblige you by getting seriously wounded! I must confess that there would have been much to be said in favour of the pellet having been another ¼ [inch] nearer, as I should then have come <u>home</u> with a broken arm – a calamity I would have got over.

We are all going very strong at present, plenty to eat and very little soap and water, so what more could anyone want? I have been in great luck the last few days, getting three or four letters a day from various people, and some **caramels** from mother. I was the most popular officer in the Regiment that day!

No doubt the Old Snake has arrived by now. Don't you give the poor old man your filthy second best chair covers in the library: His coat is green with <u>age</u>, not dirt.

Cooper, the only other officer left in my company had a letter from his butler today, which read as follows, "The family are all well but for a few fleas so are the dogs." I hope my family are not similarly afflicted as I have found out it is most unpleasant. The other day – three weeks or so ago – I sat with the Company in the middle of a turnip field, with the enemy's shells screaming over head and I was forced to take off my shirt and catch three fleas in it! This is a fact, not fiction!

I am glad to hear that Nance is so much better; now that you have done her out of her job, I will dance the grand chain with her yet. Also, I was delighted to hear that Jack had enlisted, and Collins and North volunteered for Service abroad. Tell any village people you see that I consider them all sweeps if they don't make <u>all</u> their menfolk either enlist, or if they are already terriers go abroad. I am sorry John (thin John) has not recovered enough yet to come. Give my love to Nance, Mumbo and thank Nelly for her message, and everybody. I am delighted to hear from Sibyl that she is having a holiday from S.S. [Sunday School] I wonder!

As I write I can hear the Devil of a battle going on between the french and germans miles away, though the germans in front of us - not 400 yds away - are very quiet today. I seem to have written the deuce of a letter, and now I intend fitting in an hour's sleep, as that is the only thing we lack here.

Best love
from Freddy Longman

P.S. Who is "Mr Freddy". My letter appears to be addressed to him, but I know him not.

[N.B. Louisa Ricket was the senior housemaid with the Longman family and worked there for many years. Freddy was very close to her from childhood.]

(Letter to May Oakley)

At the Front
October 2 1914

Dear Cousin May,

Ever so many thanks for your letter, which I was delighted to get – most touched in fact -. You must have been having a bad time if Louisa has been getting at you on the subject of my iniquities. I know she bores her own nieces and nephews with them, but it is hard that she should get at my own cousin too.

I am glad that that dog has thought fit to be amiable to you. He had his "dib" took the other day and mother sent me one. I gather that he too had been making everyone's life hideous by rushing violently down steep places and barking, whenever fat John or a marauding gardener approached the house.

I fear my "sufferin'" family have had an anxious day or two, as that fat headed and loathly War Office reported me "missing", when I only had the slightest flesh wound in the arm.

I cant give you any interesting news, or it would be censored, and old war news must be very wearisome. It is an unpleasant business and the sooner it is over the better. I have no objection to devoting an otherwise useless career to slaying the coney or the partridge, but I can raise no animosity against the peaceful clean looking German, who does not do the atrocities the papers say he does – if he can help it – and I resent even more performing the role of running deer, or bobbing man for his benefit.

On reading through this epistle I seem to have written a great lot of nonsense, and there are at least five words whose spelling I have tossed for. This is not a fair proportion as the most careful examination of your letter only produced one (me sister's name).
Your affect. cousin
F. Longman

P.S. I am ashamed to say I have forgotten your address and so I am sending this home.

(Letter to W Longman)

4th Bn Royal Fusiliers
Expeditionary Force
October 4 1914

My dear Fox

Many thanks for your letter and books. I have had Pickwick, Woman in White, and Scott Vol I, up to date. These will keep me good for some time, as I find one has very little time for reading except when we have short Rest periods, and then I seem to sleep all the time. I would give my boots to see you all drilling! I wonder how much drill you have to do. I bet Murton makes a goat of himself. It is sad that India is "orfli", though it has advantages, as I intend being home for Xmas. Mrs B's moustache does not sound appetising either in colour (sandy) or shape (straggly) (damn you), but no doubt she is exceedingly busy: I must send her - and the W.O. – a p.c. I heard from Susan yesterday, who tells me you are to be caught for walnut gathering. Be warned by the sad fate of my trousers the year before last; walnuts are capital things in their place, but their place is not the seat of your trousers.

I also hear your coin cabinets have arrived. This is rather exciting, but I know quite well it will mean that you do not stir outside the house on week-ends, unless these drills make you.
Y.L.b.
F. Longman
[Your Loving brother]

**4th Bn. Royal Fusiliers, Expeditionary Force
October 4 1914 (Received Oct 10)**

My dear Maw,

I have just received a packet of letters from all over the place, re-ward, etc; including some parcels of yours. According to your numbers, I have got all up to date. I was a man of some importance the day the chocolate and caramels arrived; the caramels especially being appreciated, as we can get chocolate here from time to time.

I am rather interested to know how long
1.   my letters take to get home? and
2.   how long official post cards take, and
3.   if they take roughly the same time?

Letters from home take about 8 days when the post is running regularly, though of course sometimes we do not get any letters for several days.

The day after tomorrow our company has its "post card day". They have started a plan whereby about twice a month each company has three postcards which go straight back in 36 hours, with the King's messages. Cooper and I each collar one, on which we put the company's wants, and then use (what's left) for private "porpoises". On the 3rd card we send a roll of married N.C.O.s and men present with the company. So this postcard will arrive before you get this letter.

I wrote to Sammy's father and also Mead's some days ago, so I hope by now that they have heard all that is known about their sons at present. I did not mention that Fred's hospital had been blown up. It really is abominable that they should not let these people know the Mons and Cambrai casualties yet.

They do not send us any names as killed unless some responsible person actually saw them dead, but I fear that there is only a very, very slender chance that any of the people you mention are still living; recent rumours of Fred are more hopeful on the other hand.

We have left the trenches and are treking again now; where we are I must not say, and where we are going I have no idea. I am surprised that you can make out my journal, I wonder if you can read the names of places? Thanks ever so much for copying it out, it must be an awful undertaking.

I want you to keep a "William" of the properties I write for, as many of the things on my postcards are given to the company, and the list of my wants is growing immense. All the parcels up to date have been just what was wanted.

I like my blue and white spotty hankies, and am keeping them, and presenting some white ones I had

stored in my 35 lbs kit to the needy. We have at last got our kits for a day or two, a very rare event indeed. This is a very dull letter, but really there is very little happening at present of interest and what there is I cannot write, so there it is.

> With best love to all
> Your loving son,
> F. Longman

P.S. Tell that dog that I will trouble him not to knock down and bite my Uncle Snakey this time.

P.P.S. It is possible you may not get any more letters for some little time. Posts are rarer on this trek.

(Postcard to Susan Minet)

At the Front October 6. 1914

Dear Susan,

Many thanks for your letter. I will try to P.C. the war office, but I doubt if I could compose one suitable for the occasion. I have just got a temporary job as Railway Transport Officer for a few days. This is a poor job, with plenty of work and plenty of cursing and I shall be glad when it is over and I can return to the Regiment. I have been able however to lay in a lot of supplies for the Mess when I get back.

What bad luck of St John's! I wonder if he will be out here at all. Just at present our movements are specially secret so news is scarce, but we are in a particularly beautiful part of the country, and it seems a monstrous shame to fight in it. They ought to have a "Ring" somewhere, like S. Africa, where there should be no inhabitants to turn out, and no country to spoil. A town which has been shelled for 20 days is a depressing object to go through, but I think a battered wood is an even more mournful and forlorn looking object.

I am delighted that Sibyl has finalised her writing and intends to take it easy for a bit, but I wonder if she will? Show her your two cousinly thumbs if she doesn't. Also I hear that Mary is doing wholesome occupations for a change, looking after unemployed, and especially soldier's families.

When I looked through my diary before sending it off, I had the greatest difficulty in reading it, so I think it is a wonderful performance of Mother's and Sibyl's to copy it out!

Y. A. 1st C.
F. Longman

[Yours affectionate 1st cousin]

(Postcard to Mary Minet)

Somewhere near the front.
October 7 1914

Dear Aunt Mary,

Many thanks for your P.C.s and the socks. The latter were most acceptable in the company, as home-knitted ones last so much better than others; also most of their socks have gone and only darns remain!

I wrote a P.C. to Susan a day or two ago saying I had got a job as Railway Transport Officer. That came to an end yesterday evening, since when I have been in the train with a little party of men on my own, trying to rejoin the Regiment.

We arrived at this place some hours ago, and here I have been able to refit from some large and good shops there are. I have fitted out a most luxurious hamper of potted meats, sauces, milk, etc. etc. for the mess.

I had collected a little hoard of German trophies, such as shells, heavy gun cartridges, and rifle and some bayonettes, but I am sorry to say they all had to be left behind, or I thought Geoff would have approved of some of them, no doubt I shall soon get hold of some more.

It is just possible that the absence of misspelt words from my diary may be due to the fact that mother copied part of it. The part that Sibyl copied is harder to explain.

Y.L.n.
F.Longman

Express postcard [to parents]

October 10 1914
(Received Oct 14 1914)

This postcard is Company property, so first of all will you send to the O.C. D. Company, 4th Royal Fusiliers Expeditionary Force, 10/- of cigarette papers, once a month and book it to me.

It is to be hoped that this will get home in 36 hours but I have my doubts.

We are all well and very flourishing and we have not a gun fired in anger for some time. I have written all the news that is considered wholesome for us to send, so I will not attempt to give any here: except one story which I feel some must be true! "Some of our fellows were attacking a strongly entrenched German position. It was very open ground so they could not advance by day. Each night however they dug a trench a little nearer the enemy until at last they were within 60 yds of them. They could easily shout insults at each other, and all day our own fellows tried all sorts of dodges to make them show their heels, but the Deutcher was too wily. At last an officer shouted in a peremptory voice "Waiter", when 23 heads at once popped up. "An honest fact"! I have sent a list of wants in my last letter, but I am putting the important ones here too: this does not mean I want two of them. A pair of heavy greased shooting boots tipped and heeled with metal, from Maxwells, Dover Street. The other things I want soon – as my collars and ties are gone – are two ordinary hunting stocks, khaki coloured, size 15½ and 2 do, size 16½, also cheap gold safety pins for do.

Someone has sent me a Shetland hand-knitted sweater, who I don't know. This is A.1., and just what I wanted. The one Loo gave me is still going strong, but is rather stretched, also 2 are better than one. If you know who sent it please thank them now and in 6 weeks time I will, if you tell me who it was.

Next time anyone is near Maddox Street, Bond Street, will they go to Palmers and tell them to send Mr Steele's boots at once, as his no longer exist.

Y.L.S. F. Longman

P.S. Will you also send to O.C.D Coy, 2 dozen flint and steel lighters.

Postcard [to parents]

October 14 1914
(Received 20th October 1914)

Just time for a hurried scrawl to say all is well. I had a slight contretemps the other day, when I fell into a manure water tank up to my waist. All my clothes had to be washed, and when my servant had done, he proceeded to fall in himself. The culminating misfortune was that most of my trouser buttons came off in the washing.

No time for more at present, I will try to get a letter off soon.

Y.L.S.
F Longman

(Letter to Mary Minet)

On active Service.
October 15 1914
(Hadham Hall Nov 2 1914)

My dear Aunt Mary,

Thanks ever so much for the Shetland sweater which arrived 3 days ago, and your various letters and P.C.s, all of which were very welcome. I quite agree with Ambrose on the subject of letters and I must say I have done very well.

We had not had a letter mail for some days until this morning, when I got no less than 14 letters, etc! including one from Joe, saying he hopes to get out in an armoured Rolls!

I heard about the Infant Clothing books and clothes; it is kind of the Belgian infant to come and wear them for you.

We all find my "Pickwick" invaluable, if we happen to be hungry we read of Trundle's Wedding Breakfast;

if we are hot, the Shooting Lunch does very well, and the Xmas dinner when it is cold, and so on.

We have just been reinforced by 10 officers, and one of them who has come to our company has got a little pocket Calverly, with the exam papers, and I was disgusted to have to plough himself; however, I have just censored one of our men's letters to Goswell Street which has made a good deal of difference.

We have got a most invaluable cook in the company. We are messing by companies now and I run our company mess and turned on the mess waiter to cook, when to my joy I find that he is a born artist! He makes first rate suet puddings, apple dumplings and pastry, out of flour and bacon fat.

The leaves are coming off fast here, but the colours are very disappointing; most of the leaves seem to come off green. This convinces me in my idea that foreign parts are very inferior to England after all.

There is plenty of news, though not too exciting, which I cannot send.

Your loving nephew,
F. Longman

P.S. 7 pairs of socks just arrived, which were eagerly snapped by the men. All the men who have been with us all the time are now resocked, and we are beginning on reinforcements. Many thanks for them to the makers. F.L.

On Active Service
October 15 1914
(Received November 2 1914)

My dear Mother and Father,

Many thanks for the letters and parcels which arrived today. We had not had any letters for some days, and when they did come I had a record mail, including one from Mr and Miss Pills, Joe Brooks and others. This was very cheery. When all the warm things that I have written for, or have been sent me are here, I should have the laugh of any ordinary polar bear.

We have just been reinforced by 11 officers, nine in one draft, one from the ranks, and one yesterday from England. This brings us nearly up to full strength again, and owing to the small rooms we get in most of our billets necessitates Company messes. I am running it at present and luckily we have got an excellent cook in the Company. He turns out the most wonderful dishes out of the rations, we get helped by a small hamper that I collected on the way here. Yesterday we had some apple dumplings that would have done justice to fat Anne! [Anne Ward – the family cook] The supplies you have ordered will be a most welcome addition to our hamper.

Anne Ward – cook to the Longman family (1899)

I have just got a new pack. It is technically known as a "sac-de-chasse" and is rather like a shooting edition of my fishing bag, only much more roomy. This fits on my back as if made to fit it and will be most useful. At present it weighs about a ton, as it is packed with food and woollies which I have not been able to put in my valise yet. However "I am pretty tough and that's one comfort as the very old turkey said."

The new officers include many nice ones and a few rather rum. The type of fellow we are getting as reinforcements is, in many cases, very different from the regular officer. Many of them talk a very new language, in one case. - and that in our Company - not half as good as most of our N.C.Os. This is rather a pity, as of course we want the very best we can get just now. This may be unreasonable, as no doubt they are just as good officers, but it is not so nice in the mess. Whilst on the grouse, I am thinking of sending a P.C. to the War Office. There have been vacancies for about six weeks above Beazley and myself, and they have only just promoted Beazley and not yet me. This is slightly annoying, as officers coming up from the Special Reserve most of them have got their second and so all come in senior to me, and as at the end of the war, they have the option of staying on, I imagine they will remain senior.

From the fact of my having time for all this grousing you will guess that we are not having as strenuous a time as we have had.

Our new Captain is Sir Francis Waller, who used to be in the Rgt. but left some years ago. I believe he is no relation to our Wallers, but he is related to the Towers of Weald Hall. He seems to be a very good bird.

I will ask the Adjutant for leave to shoot on the 3rd, but it is possible he may not grant it; however, I generally turn up at least one train before expected, so you never know.

Best love to all,
Your loving son
F. Longman

This was to be the final letter Freddy sent home. He was killed three days later.

The following poem, entitled the Last Post was found amongst his mother's papers. It was published in the *Spectator Magazine* on 20th November 1915 and very effectively recounts the importance of receiving news from the front.

LAST POST

LAST summer, centuries ago,
I watched the postman's lantern glow,
As night by night on leaden feet
He twinkled down our darkened street.

So welcome on his beaten track,
The bent man with the bulging sack!
But dread of every sleepless couch,
A whistling imp with leathern pouch!

And now I meet him in the way,
And earth is Heaven, night is Day,
For oh! there shines before his lamp
An envelope without a stamp!

Address in pencil; overhead,
The Censor's triangle in red.
Indoors and up the stair I bound:
"One from the boy, still safe, still sound!

"Still merry in a dubious trench
They've taken over from the French;
Still making light of duty done;
Still full of Tommy, Fritz, and fun!

"Still finding War of games the cream,
And his platoon a priceless team -
Still running it by sportsman's rule,
Just as he ran his house at school.

"Still wild about the ' bombing stunt'
He makes his hobby at the front.
Still trustful of his wondrous luck -
'Prepared to take on old man Kluck!'"

Awed only in the peaceful spells,
And only scornful of their shells,
His beaming eye yet found delight
In ruins lit by flares at night,

In clover field and hedge-row green,
Apart from cover or a screen,
In Nature spurting spick-and-span
For all the devilries of Man.

He said those weeks of blood and tears
Were worth his score of radiant years.
He said he had not lived before –
Our boy who never dreamt of War!

He gave us of his own dear glow,
Last summer, centuries ago.
Bronzed leaves still cling to every bough.
I don't waylay the postman now.

Doubtless upon his nightly beat
He still comes twinkling down our street.
I am not there with straining eye –
A whistling imp could tell you why.

E. W. H.

SACRIFICE

On 18th October 1914, Freddy Longman was killed at Herlies in northern France. The following words attempt to capture the impact this had on his family, his friends and neighbours, and his military colleagues.

On 21st October 1914, a telegram was received by the post office in Braughing and hurriedly delivered to Freddy's family at Upp Hall. The horrors of war were to become all too evident for the Archer family at the village post office, who had the unenviable job of delivering this devastating news to Freddy's and other families. This was to be the first of those devastating life changing messages. The following was the stark content of that very telegram.

POST OFFICE TELEGRAM FROM WAR OFFICE
21st October 1914

To C.J. Longman Esq Upp Hall Braughing Herts

Deeply regret to inform you that 2nd Lieut F Longman Royal Fusiliers was killed in action on 18 October Lord Kitchener expresses his sympathy.

FROM Secretary, War Office.

Telegram informing the family of the death of Freddy

The Royal Fusiliers in the Great War by H.C. O'Neill published in 1922 describes the circumstances surrounding the death of Freddy Longman (p 51-52).

On October 12th the 4th Battalion moved towards Vieille Chapelle along roads almost blocked by French cavalry. They were in divisional reserve, and remained so until 15th, when they moved forward towards the Estaires-Neuve Chapelle road. The battalion attacked through Pont du Hem, W and X Companies being in the front line; and easily brushed aside the cavalry screen in front of them. The advance was resumed on the following day to the Rue d'Enfer, where the enemy were found holding houses, and at dusk a halt was made on a line extending from Trivolet, ... along Rue d'Enfer, to Moulin du Pietre. .... There had been little resistance, and the few casualties suffered were due to snipers.

Herlies. – Aubers had been evacuated during the night, and the battalion entered it unopposed on the morning of the 17th; but there some German cavalry were encountered advancing from Fromelles. The battalion was on the left of the division, with its flank supposed to be covered by French cavalry. The advance of the German cavalry delayed the march upon Herlies, which was found to be held in some strength. Captain Swift, with W Company, marched direct upon it by the Aubers-Herlies road, while Colonel McMahon took the other three companies through Le Plouich and Le Riez. The Lincolns, on the right of the Fusiliers, moved due eastwards; and under this converging attack the Germans were forced out of the village. At about 6.30 p.m. Colonel McMahon entered from the north as Swift, with the Lincolns, was pushing the enemy out at the point of the bayonet. W Company lost Lieutenant Hodges, killed, and about 10 other casualties. An outpost line was taken up from Le Petit Riez to the southern outskirts of Herlies. The houses were searched, and a few Germans were discovered.

The division had now reached an uneasy equilibrium with the German forces on their front, and no further advance was possible. The 18th was spent in strengthening the positions, all of which came under a heavy bombardment from field and heavy guns. About 5 p.m. the battalions on the right and left of the Royal Fusiliers, the Scots Fusiliers and the Royal Irish, attacked after a preliminary bombardment. The Germans at once replied. Captain Waller, Lieutenants Cooper, Gorst and Longman, all of Z Company, were at this time having tea in a farm at Petit Riez, near their trenches. The three first ran out to see what was happening. Longman stayed behind; and a shell fell upon the farm, burst in the room and killed him as he sat at a table, a tragic end to a life of much promise.

De Ruvigny's Roll of Honour 1914 to 1924

This publication contains the biographies of over 26,000 casualties of the Great War. Often including further details provided by families, the entry for Freddy Longman tells a slightly different version of events leading to his death.

'.....gazetted 2nd Lieut., Royal Fusiliers, 13 Feb. 1912 and promoted Lieut. 24 Aug. 1914; went to France 13th August; was wounded in the arm at the Battle of Marne, but rejoined his regt. after a short stay at a base hospital, and was killed in action at Herlies, 18 Oct. .... On this day his regiment was holding the village of Le Riez close to Herlies and he was resting in a farm with some brother officers, when a shell burst over this house. Lieut. Longman ran to put on his equipment and join his men; but another shell exploded just outside the window and a pellet struck him in the temple, killing him instantaneously......'

23rd October 1914 – The Private Diaries of Sir Henry Rider Haggard (p 11)

On this day, the author Rider Haggard made the following entry in his diary:

'Freddie Longman of the Royal Fusiliers the son of my old friend Charles Longman, has been killed. We knew the poor boy well, and he has stayed here; he was a charming young man, and took great interest in all that had to do with his profession. At the commencement of the war he was slightly wounded and got four bullets through his clothes. After a short time in hospital in France he rejoined his regiment, and now he is gone. I fear his family will be desolated, for he was their idol. Such is War.'

23rd October 1914 – *The Times*
THE FALLEN OFFICERS

'...... Lieutenant Frederick Longman, 4th Battalion Royal Fusiliers, who was killed in action on October 18, was the second son of Mr Charles James Longman, of Upp Hall, Braughing, a member of the publishing firm Longmans, Green and Co. He was 24 years of age, and was educated at Harrow and Pembroke College, Cambridge. He was a good football player, boxer, swimmer, and rifle shot. While at Harrow he was an active member of the school corps, and at Cambridge of the University O.T.C. In 1910 he received a commission in the Hertfordshire Territorial Regiment. He was an energetic member of the Braughing Rifle Club, and gave much time to training lads from the village at the miniature range, some of whom became excellent shots. He was gazetted to the Royal Fusiliers in August 1912, and was wounded at the battle of the Marne, but recovered quickly and rejoined his regiment.'

23rd October 1914

Walter P.H. Hill sent a letter of condolence to Freddy's mother.

Royal Military College
Camberley
Surrey
23.10.14

Dear Mrs Longman,

I write to express to you my deep sympathy in the loss of your gallant son. I was the adjutant of the 4th Battalion when he joined, so I knew him well. Being a quiet & unassuming sort, it took his brother officers some time to discover what a really fine character he had. I unfortunately was not present when he fought in the Southern Command Boxing Meeting, but Capt. Campbell of the Gordons who is one of the army's most expert judges, told me that his fight was the finest thing that he had ever seen, and he held it up to the men as an example of British pluck and endurance. A crowded house cheered him to the echo. His boxing troop put up a splendid show, entirely due to his energy and care. From this we all saw that he was a boy to be noted and one who would make as valuable Regimental Officer as it was possible to find.

He had grown steadily in popularity with his brother officers, and his cheery way had endeared him to his men. He was one of those responsible for the fine work of the Battalion, which brought down Gen'l Sir John French's splendid praise.

"Your country & myself are proud of you and no Battalion in the world could have done better."

He has died a glorious death and his life as what I saw of it was that of a clean minded English Gentleman. This must help you to bear his loss, which by the results gained has not been in vain. The Regiment have lost a brave comrade who we shall miss, but of whom we are all proud.

In deepest sympathy
Sincerely Yours
Walter P.H. Hill

27th October 1914

The following is a letter from Freddy's sister, Sibyl to her cousin Margaret Puller, who lived at Youngsbury in Ware:

Upp Hall
Braughing
Ware
October 27th 1914

Dearest Margaret,

Yesterday I could not thank you for your letter – but I know you understood. The love and sympathy of you all has been a real help to each of us – for we know you too loved him, and knew how he was just all the world to us. – One can only blindly wait – but I do believe that at last – even on "this side" – & even to Father and Mother – joy will come back – though nothing can ever be the same, of course. – But when at last we win through to joy, he will seem nearest to us of all. – He helped so many, through that splendid power of joy – & because we know a bit what he must have suffered in his large hearted sympathy, for all the misery he saw – we do thank God that he is saved from it all, now that he has done his bit – which no one else might do! –

You will know, too, Margaret dear – how it makes one long for peace more than ever & yet dread unspeakably for Father & Mother the day when they will feel – "he might have come back today". – God make us all stronger by then! –

I have copied one of the letters which has helped

us most. – I love to remember Freddy's own account of his doings at that boxing match, when he came home with his knee. "Oh – I slipped & put out my knee, so was knocked out – but it would have been all the same any way, as I'd come up against the champion". –

Much love
Yrs. Sibyl L.

31st October 1914 – *Hertfordshire Mercury*
BRAUGHING
LIEUT. LONGMAN KILLED IN ACTION.

As briefly announced in last week's Mercury, Lieut. Frederick Longman of Braughing has nobly laid down his life for his country, his name being among the list of officers killed in action which was published on the 22nd inst.

Lieut. Frederick Longman was the second son of Mr. Charles James Longman of Upp Hall, Braughing, a member of the publishing firm of Longmans, Green and Co. He was 24 years of age, and was educated at Harrow and Pembroke College, Cambridge. He was a good football player, boxer, swimmer and rifle shot. All his life he was an enthusiast for military training. While at Harrow he was an active member of the School Corps, and at Cambridge of the O.T.C. [Officer Training Corps]. He retired from the latter body on receiving a commission in the Hertfordshire Regiment of Territorials. At that time it was desired to raise a section of twenty-five men in Braughing. He set about it with his usual energy and recruited forty-one men. He was an energetic member of the local Rifle Club, and gave much time to training lads from the village school at the miniature range, some of whom became excellent shots. He was gazetted to the Royal Fusiliers in August 1912 and was wounded at the Battle of the Marne. On this occasion four bullets passed through his clothes, besides the one that wounded his arm. He was sent back to the base but recovered quickly and rejoined his regiment. His cheerful manners and sterling character gained him many friends and caused him to be universally loved.

12th November 1914 – The Private Diaries of Sir Henry Rider Haggard (p 14)

The author made this further entry:

'I saw Charles Longman today. Poor Freddie was killed by a shell. I did not like to pursue the subject, seeing that it distressed him beyond bearing. I thought he looked thin. The old gentlemen at the Athenaeum play their afternoon bridge as usual in the smoking-room. Probably they are wise so to do, but I admire their detachment of mind.....'

The author Henry Rider Haggard and his wife visit Upp Hall in 1899

'When the Burnt Offering Began'

Freddy's family were clearly devastated by the loss of the youngest member of their family. Found amongst other family papers was the following:

'When the burnt-offering began, the song of the LORD began also with the trumpets.'
(2 Chron xxix. 27)

> And thus can English mother yield
> Her darling up to die!
> Ere yet the shout of playing-field
> And nursery names and schoolday quip
> Of talk have faded from his lip,
> Or laughter from his eye.
>
> Of old, 'tis said, 'neath Syrian skies,
> In dumb devotion bowed,
> Men watched their whole burnt-offering rise:
> But in that moment, clear and strong,
> Outburst of trumpets and the song
> Of triumph rent the cloud.

> Ours to the altar laugh their way:
> Tear-blinded offerers we:--
> Lord of the sacrifice, to-day
> Touch and transform this grief that smarts,
> Wake song and trumpet in the hearts
> That give their best for Thee.

A Poem from Freddy

Amongst Freddy's papers that have survived there is a poem, which he may have sent to somebody at home. However, he refers to a poem he sent with a letter to Philip Pilditch on 11th August.

This poem was sent with the scribbled note attached saying:

'To pass on.

You may know it – but I always long for new scraps of strength to put in a letter (as our letters all generally go thru' "knocked"! Dear love & gratitude 2.U. & yr "Comrade"

> The ground is hard and thick with seed
> And roots of intertwining weed,
> The sky is grey, the wind is chill;
> I ask of thee keep ploughing still,
> For love of me.

> It may be much reward must wait
> Till thou has passed the pearly gate,
> It may be other hands will reap
> Where thou art ploughing furrows deep,
> For love of me.

> I ask of thee keep ploughing still
> With hopeful heart and steadfast will,
> Unheeding worldly praise or blame,
> Thy motive evermore the same,
> For love of me.

> If feet should tire, and heart should ache,
> Yet ever keep thy love awake
> With thought of how thy Saviour came,
> Endured the cross, despised the shame,
> For love of thee.

.Second Lieutenant Frederick Longman of 4th Battalion Royal Fusiliers 1914

LEST WE FORGET

There is much to remind us of Freddy Longman even today, one hundred years after his death. His family and friends have ensured he is not forgotten. The following extracts describe the various events that took place in the months and years during and after the Great War that have created a long lasting memory.

Memorial Service – St Mary's Church, Braughing

On 14 November 1914, the *Hertfordshire Mercury* published the details of a memorial service held for Freddy. It is notable how few men are listed amongst the congregation. This must have been an incredibly emotional service to remember the young man, friend and neighbour whom they had all lost, but also a stark reminder to everyone about the dangers facing their own families. This was to be the first of 23 men from Braughing to lose their lives during this war.

St Mary's Church, Braughing 1912

MEMORIAL SERVICE FOR LIEUT. FREDERICK LONGMAN

A memorial service for the late Lieut. Frederick Longman, of the 4th Battalion Royal Fusiliers, who was killed in action at Herlies in Northern France, on the 18th Ult., was held at St. Mary's Church, Braughing, on Saturday afternoon last [7th November]. Prior to the service, which was most impressive, a muffled peal was rung on the church bells. The tenor bell was only half muffled, consequently each alternate stroke was clear, and thus gave the effect of tolling. The altar was adorned with choice white flowers specially sent from Hamels Park. The family were not present, as at the same time, they attended a similar memorial service at the Latimer Road Mission, Harrow Road, London, the Mission having had a very devoted worker in the late officer.

There was a good congregation present at Braughing Church, including Major H. A. and Mrs. Anderson (Major Anderson, late of the Royal Fusiliers, represented the deceased's regiment), Mr. and Mrs. H. Shepherd Cross and Miss Shepherd Cross, Dr. and Mrs. A. W. Ewing, Mrs. Thomson, Mr. and Mrs. C. F. Mole, Mr. J. Keast, Mr. E. Lanyon, Mr. and Mrs. W. B. Murton, Mrs. Slee, Mrs. T. T. Greg, Mrs. W. Edwards, Mrs. Milton Mole, Mr. and Mrs. H. E. Salt, Mrs. A. S. Edwards, Miss. Deards, Mrs. W. Webb, Mrs. Eggleton, Miss Hawken, Mr. and Mrs. D. Mutimer, Mr. E. Kennedy, Mr. H. Robinson, Mr. Wright, Miss Smith (Pentlows), Mr. E. Martin, Miss Patten, etc.

The solemn service opened with the hymn, 'Through the night of doubt and sorrow,' and the Vicar, the Rev. L. E. Baumer, read the lesson from the Burial Service, and after the Psalm, 'Domine Refugium,' had been chanted, the concluding prayers from the same service were read, beginning with the Lesser Litany. The anthem, 'Sunset and evening star' (Rev. H. H. Woodward), from Tennyson's well-known hymn, 'Crossing the Bar,' was sung with marked expression, and gave a special solemnity to the service. The remaining prayers were taken from the form of intercession service enjoined for use during the war throughout the diocese. The Hymn 'Fight the good fight with all thy might,' was sung and the service concluded with Govier's 'Threefold Amen,' followed by singing of the National Anthem. The choir was present and Mr. E. Booth, the organist, played as a concluding voluntary Mendelssohn's 'O rest in the Lord.' The death of the popular young officer at the early age of 24 is regretted and lamented by the parish.

The Harrovian

The Harrow School magazine reported the following in relation to the Harrow Mission on 21 November 1914:

'F. Longman's death was a real blow to many of us here. He used to come to our Summer Camp, while his brother and sister have done a great deal for us. The Memorial Service for him, which we held here, was well attended, and many old Harrovians were with us for it.'

Harrow Memorials of the Great War Volume 1

Published in 1918 for Harrow School, this book contains the details of the first 100 past students known as 'Old Harrovians,' to fall in the war between August 23rd, 1914 and March 20th, 1915. The entry relating to Freddy Longman reads as follows:

LIEUTENANT F. LONGMAN

Royal Fusiliers

Rendalls 03^3-07^3 *Aged 24*   *Oct 18th 1914*

SECOND son of C.J. Longman (O.H.) [Old Harrovian] of Upp Hall, Braughing, Herts, and partner in Messrs. Longmans, Green and Co., 39 Paternoster Row, and of Harriet Ann Longman.

Football XI, 1907; Dolphin, 1907; Champion Feather-weight Boxer, 1907. Pembroke College, Cambridge.

Lieutenant Longman was killed in action on October 18th, 1914, at Herlies, in N. France. He had been previously wounded in the arm (with four other bullets through his clothes) at the Battle of the Marne; but he rejoined after a short stay in a base hospital.

His Colonel (since killed in action) wrote: ---
"Please accept my deepest sympathy and be consoled with the thought that his work on active service was as sound and valuable as his conduct has been brave and dutiful. His rapid return to duty after the wound received on crossing the Marne marked him specially as a genuine solider, and his loss will be very much felt by all of us, professionally and socially."

A brother officer writes: ----
"He was always cheery, and it did us all good to see the way he did his job, and never grumbled at anything. He was one of the gallantest fellows I ever saw, and nothing ever frightened him. We are all

proud of him, and his name will always go on in the Regiment's history as a hero."

Captain Cooper, 4th Battalion Royal Fusiliers writes: ---
"One couldn't want a more excellent companion or a braver fellow, always absolutely cool and unruffled, and the most cheery person imaginable under most trying circumstances, and I can hardly tell you what a lot this latter means on a show like this."

Captain Hill, Adjutant of the 4th Royal Fusiliers, writes: ---
"I unfortunately, was not present when he fought in the Southern Command Boxing Meeting, but Corporal Campbell of the Gordons, who is one of the Army's most expert judges, told me that his fight was the finest thing he had ever seen, and he held it up to the men as an example of British pluck and endurance. A crowded house cheered him to the echo."

War Memorial, Braughing, Hertfordshire

Freddy's father, already a parish councillor in Braughing, was elected as its chairman in 1916, a post he held until he retired in 1925. In addition he was Secretary of the War Memorial Committee 1919 – 1921. In these influential roles, he was pivotal in the development of the Braughing war memorial. Philip Pilditch, an old friend of Freddy's to whom he wrote during his brief time in France, was engaged as the architect. The memorial, unveiled in 1920, contains the names of 22 Braughing men killed in the Great War. The name of the 23rd man, Cecil Herbert Shepherd-Cross, is not recorded on the war memorial, as is appears on a memorial elsewhere, having been married and moved to London before the war.

On 31 July 1920 the *Hertfordshire Mercury* published an article about the unveiling of the war memorial:

BRAUGHING WAR MEMORIAL
Unveiled by Mr C.J. Longman

The handsome parish church of St. Mary at Braughing, was packed on Sunday [25 July] on the occasion of the unveiling of the memorial to the brave men of the village who sacrificed their lives in the great War. The front seats were reserved for the mourners, who gathered together in large numbers to

Braughing War Memorial 1920

the Vicar, the hymn "O God, our help in ages past" was sung, and prayers offered.

The Vicar took his text from St Matthew XX, 21, "Ye know not what ye ask." He described, as related in this passage of scripture, how the mother of Zebedee's children asked our Lord that her two sons, James and John, might sit, the one on His right hand and the other on His left, in His kingdom. The speaker told this wonderful story to his hearers, unfolding the history of the lives and martyrdom of those two apostles, St. James and St. John. The history of St James, he said 'brings home to us the family phenomenon of a precious life, early shortened, a burning spirit suddenly quenched, a large and brave heart early laid to rest, the goodly promise of early manhood all unfulfilled, the work which he longed to do left uncompleted. Why was it, how is it, how can it be? Such questions will never be fully answered. Only when the shadows flee away and there shall be no room for further question. He could only venture to suggest that Christ has work for each to-day, and He Himself

FINISHED HIS GREAT WORK

in three short years, it may very well happen that at the end of a very short period of probation it may please Him to dispense with the services of any of His faithful soldiers and to take them to Himself. "And this thought", he said, "must to-day perforce be transferred to the annals of our private experience. Why was it, how is it, how can it be? How often has this question come to our minds during the War? How they must be in the minds of all here this afternoon. As St. John the Baptist was slain at the instigation of a dancing girl, so the very flower of this nation's manhood have been killed in battle or have died of their wounds to satisfy the demands of a brutal materialism and of a tyrannical military authority. Yet even we blind mortals can see that these men have not died in vain. For it is as a libation at the altar that all these tears and blood have been poured out, and these young lives sacrificed.

pay a last and solemn tribute to those men near and dear to them. The parishioners proceeded to church to the sound of a muffled peal of bells, and here and there was to be seen the Union Jack at half-mast.

When the service commenced people were standing in the aisles and porch consequent upon the seating capacity of the church being so taxed, and the hymn "Through the night of doubt and sorrow" was sung, following which the Vicar (the Rev. E.J. Baker), who conducted the service, read introductory sentences. The psalm, "The Lord is my Shepherd" was chanted, and the lesson, read by the Congregational Minister (the Rev. W. J. Hailstone) was taken from Solomon III, 1-8. Prior to the address by

We have met together to dedicate a memorial to those who have so fallen. A monument of singular beauty. Let this memorial keep green in our hearts those whose names are recorded on its panels of honour. Oh, let us never forget them! Surely it is a sacred duty to continue to love the dead, who have been dear to us here on earth. And perhaps we owe them something else than love. We may owe them penitence. How often have we been in the wrong regarding them. How have we vexed or distressed them by our unkindness or obstinacy or at the best by our thoughtlessness. All these things should make us ready and eager to anticipate

THAT AFTER MEETING

with them when all that was wrong has been forgiven. We may learn to avoid with the living the mistakes we made with the dead. Let us think how we have been perverse or unkind to some dear one, father or mother, husband or wife, sister or brother, even to sons or daughters, and to determine that no such like shall occur again. Let us hold on to the end when, in due time, the shadows shall pass away, the veil will be drawn aside, and we shall be made one again in our heavenly Father's realm."

The congregation then proceeded to the site of the memorial, which is situate at the end of the road leading to the church, walking in the following order: - Demobilized soldiers (about 60 in number); children of the parish; choir and clergy and the general congregation. On arrival the hymn "For all the Saints" was sung, and then the Chairman of the Parish Council, Mr. C.J. Longman, unveiled the memorial, reading the inscription as under:

"This cross commemorates the twenty-two gallant men of Braughing who died for their king and country in the great War waged for the cause of Freedom by England and her Allies during the years 1914 to 1918."

At the reading of each name a wreath or other floral tribute was placed at the foot of the cross by the mourners, presenting a very suggestive tribute. The names inscribed are as follows: John Baldwin, John William Ball, Frederick George Bunce, Arthur John Cannon, Alderman Clark, Charles Collins, William Herbert Cook, Ramah Deville, John Dickerson, Frederick James Harvey Furneaux, William Hamilton, Charles Lewis, Frederick Longman, Robert Arthur Cyril Nash, Herbert Reginald Parker, Robert

Rogers, William John Skipp, Arthur Smith, George Victor Taylor, Frederick Whyman, Ernest Wren and Thomas Wright.

The Vicar then offered prayers of dedication, etc. and the service closed with the Benediction.

Sergt. Carpenter, Instructor of the Hertford Grammar School O.T.C., [Officer Training Centre] sounded the "Last Post." Unfortunately, the rain had poured down during the whole of the service, but did not interfere greatly with the proceedings.

The handsome memorial, which was sculptured and erected by Messrs. Peck Bros., of Hertford, takes the form of a grey rustic Cornish granite cross with die and base, standing about 13 feet high. A bronze metal medallion "Hart" is let in the centre of the cross, and the four metal panels containing the names and inscription with letters of same in relief are let into the die.

The cross was designed by Mr. P. H. Pilditch, of the firm of Pilditch, Chadwick and Co, of Old Bond Street, London W.1."

Stained Glass Window, St Mary's Church, Braughing, Hertfordshire

At the east end of the south aisle of the fifteenth century nave of this church, Freddy's parents commissioned the design and installation of a beautiful stained glass window in memory of their son. This was erected in 1920 and contains large images of three gallant soldiers from various stages of history:

Godfrey de Bouillon, a medieval knight and crusader and brother of Eustace Count of Boulogne who held land in Braughing; Godfrey joined the First Crusade in 1096 and became Ruler of Jerusalem until his unexpected death in 1100.

St George, who served as an officer in the Roman army, protested against the torture of Christians and was executed in 303 AD for his beliefs.

Charles Gordon, born in 1833 in London and commissioned in 1852 as a second lieutenant in the Royal Engineers and promoted to lieutenant in 1854. He saw action in the Crimean War, in China and in Africa. He was promoted to the rank of Major

General in 1882 and was murdered during a revolt in Khartoum, Sudan in 1885.

The window also contains a range of imagery pertinent to Freddy's including images of small animals, loved so much by him as a child.

On 4 September 1920 the *Hertfordshire Mercury* published details of the window:

DEDICATION OF MEMORIAL WINDOW. ------ A beautifully designed stained glass window executed by an eminent London firm, has been presented to St. Mary's Church, Braughing, by Mr. and Mrs. C. J. Longman, of Upp Hall, in memory of their second son, Lieut. Frederick Longman, 4th Battalion Royal Fusiliers, who fell at Herlies, Northern France, on October 18 1914.

He was the first Braughing soldier that fell in the war. The window, which is at the east end of the south aisle, is a worthy memorial to a gallant soldier, and adds a beautiful feature of adornment to the church. It was dedicated on Sunday afternoon last [29 August] at a well attended special service conducted by the vicar, the Rev. E. J. Baker.

The processional hymn was "Fight the good fight," when the choir proceeded to the end of the south aisle, where the Vicar read the dedicatory service. The special psalm chanted was "The Lord is our light" and other responses, lesson from Isaiah LIV [54], verses 11 to 14, prayers and a most appropriate dedicatory prayer. The Vicar said, "In the faith of Jesus Christ we dedicate this window to the glory of God and in memory of his servant Frederick Longman, in the name of the Father and of the Son, and of the Holy Ghost. Amen." The hymn following was, "In our day of thanksgiving one psalm let us offer for the Saints who before us have found their reward."

After the concluding prayers of the service and the blessing, the recessional hymn "Through the night of doubt and sorrow," was fervently sung. Miss Cannon, who presided at the organ, played as a concluding voluntary, Mendelssohn's "O rest in the Lord."

Following this event, an article was published in the Braughing Parish Magazine in October 1920,

The Longman memorial window in St Mary's Church, Braughing

which gave some further details about the window, which are worthy of inclusion:

On Sunday, August 29th, 1920, a Service was held in the Church for the Dedication of the Window at the East End of the South aisle, which has been filled with stained glass in memory of the late Lieut. Frederick Longman, 4th Battn. Royal Fusiliers, who fell in action at Herlies, in N. France, on October 18th, 1914, aged 24. The window has been designed by Mr. Robert Anning Bell, A.R.A., and the glass has been made by Messrs. Lowndes and Drury, of Lettice Street, Fulham.

Lieut. F. Longman was educated at Harrow

School, and at Pembroke College, Cambridge, and was from childhood devoted to outdoor life and sports and natural history. He was a good boxer, a fine swimmer and a good rifle shot, and these pursuits helped him, on joining the Royal Fusiliers, to enter keenly into the daily life and amusements of his men, by whom he was greatly loved.

The call to active service came when he had been a soldier but for a couple of years. He had time enough, however, to be trained to become a capable officer in the small but highly efficient British Army. After two and a half strenuous months, during which he was wounded and returned to duty (receiving one bullet through his arm and four through his clothes), he fell gallantly fighting for his King and Country.

The design of the window is intended to be typical of such as career as this. At the top of the north light of the window Mr. Anning Bell has worked in a little sketch of Upp Hall, the much loved Hertfordshire home from which the lad had set out on his life's work. The dome of St. Paul's Cathedral in the centre recalls the fact that Lieut. Longman was born in London and that the Royal Fusiliers is the City of London Regiment. At the top of the south light is a hint of the Heavenly City, the final goal, and resting place to which all true soldiers hope whether soon or late, to come home at last.

The figures which occupy the three lights typify the ideals of a young soldier. In the centre, St. George, the patron saint of England, is shewn killing the Dragon, a legendary feat which may be taken to be emblematic of the victory of right over might, of good faith over falsehood, won by the Allies in the Great War. On St. George's right stands Godfrey de Bouillon, a warrior of stainless integrity, one of the leaders of the First Crusade, who for this bravery and his virtues was chosen to be King of Jerusalem. Gordon, who fills the third light, by his noble life did more than any man in recent times to recall to the younger generation the ideals of the Soldier Saints of the middle ages, and to foster that spirit of devotion to duty which brought us the victory.

The heraldic devices worked into the lower part of the window and the sides of the lights are connected with the scenes of Lieut. Longman's life. The arms of

Harrow School, of the City of London, of Pembroke College and of the University of Cambridge, may be recognised. The Hertfordshire Hart is also there, the badge of the Royal Fusiliers, St. George's Cross and the Ship and Black Swan, the ancient device of his father's firm in Paternoster Row.

Golden Book of Braughing

IN this book are written the names of the men of BRAUGHING who served in the forces of King George Vth. in the war which broke out on the 4th. of August 1914, and the names of those who offered themselves for service.

In the year 1911, the Parish of Braughing in the county of Herts contained 949 souls in all, reckoning men, women & children. Of this number 128 men served, & 7 more offered their services, but owing to lack of health or strength these 7 could not gain their desire to serve their country in arms. Of the 128 men who joined the forces of the King, twenty-two died gloriously, giving their lives to preserve the freedom of their country & the honour of their King. The names of these twenty-two gallant men are recorded on a stone Cross erected in Braughing Parish where the road forks a little to the north of Ford bridge over the River Rib. The names of all who served, or who offered themselves for service, are recorded in this book, as an example to those who come after, so that should our beloved England ever again be hard pressed by enemies this record of the deeds of the men who fought in the War of 1914, may help the men then living in Braughing Parish to do their duty in like manner as their forefathers did. Should such an occasion arise, which may God forbid, or should any men of Braughing render to their country service of any kind worthy of being recorded, then the blank leaves at the end of this book afford a space where the record may be made.

Introduction to the Golden Book of Braughing

Charles Longman continued to use his connections to design and produce a wonderful memorial in the form of a beautiful leather bound book dedicated to all 128 men who joined the armed forces during the Great War including the 22 men who paid the ultimate sacrifice. Specially designed questionnaires were completed by soldiers or their families following the end of the war and the information received was used to create this rare commemoration.

The Hertfordshire Mercury records on 8th January 1921:

GOLDEN BOOK. ---- The Golden Book, the gift to the parish by Mr. C .J. Longman, will be a very treasured war memorial, and a worthy addition to the handsome memorial cross erected in the village by the parishioners. It is a book of singular beauty, and contains a brief biographical sketch of all Braughing men that served in the Great War. The names of all are written in red, and the particulars respecting the 22 men who fell in War are also similarly recorded. The volume is beautifully executed, and illuminated by a skilled writer, and recalls the artistic manuscript books of bygone times. The book has been placed on an old oak Bible desk at the end of the north aisle of the parish church, and can be readily inspected. There are a number of spare pages, so that any striking events in the parish can in future be recorded and perpetuated.

Campaign Medals

In February 1921, Charles Longman was to receive the campaign medals he had applied for on behalf of his son Freddy.

1914 Star

A bronze medal award for those who had served in France and Belgium between 5th August 1914 to midnight on 22nd November 1914. It is a medal given to those responsible for assisting the French to hold back the German army while new recruits could be trained and equipped. The medal recognises the part they played in the first sixteen weeks of the Great War. There were approximately 378,000 1914 Stars issued.

British War Medal

A silver medal awarded to officers and men of the British and Imperial Forces who either entered a

1914 Star awarded posthumously to Freddy for his service in France in the early days of the Great War

British War and Victory Medals

theatre of war or entered service overseas between 5th August 1914 and 11th November 1918. Approximately 6.5 million British War Medals were issued.

Allied Victory Medal

Awarded by each of the allies, a bronze medal with similar design and identical ribbon. Approximately 5.7 million victory medals were issued.

Memorial Plaque and Scroll

Designed during the war, production began in January 1919 and were sent to the next of kin of all soldiers who died between 4th August 1914 and 30th April 1919 whilst in military service. Freddy's plaque and scroll were sent to his parents and have survived.

BUCKINGHAM PALACE.

I join with my grateful people in sending you this memorial of a brave life given for others in the Great War.

George R.I.

Cover letter from HM King George V sent with Memorial Plaque and Scroll of families of those killed in action

Gv RI

HE whom this scroll commemorates was numbered among those who, at the call of King and Country, left all that was dear to them, endured hardness, faced danger, and finally passed out of the sight of men by the path of duty and self-sacrifice, giving up their own lives that others might live in freedom. Let those who come after see to it that his name be not forgotten.

Lieut. Frederick Longman
Royal Fusiliers

Memorial Scroll for Lieutenant Frederick Longman

Letter from Sir Godfrey Thomas

Sir Godfrey John Vignoles Thomas was a year older than Freddy and also attended Harrow School. He entered the diplomatic service before the Great War and in 1914 was based at the British Embassy in Berlin. In 1919 he became Private Secretary to the Prince of Wales, later King Edward VIII. Although offered the job of Private Secretary to the King in 1936, he declined and became Private Secretary to the Duke of Gloucester until 1957. He was provided with a grace and favour apartment at St James Palace, from where this letter was written.

March 17, 1924
ST JAMES'S PALACE, S.W.

Dear Mrs Longman,

I got back last week from a months leave abroad and found the parcel waiting at my flat. I hope when you got no reply you realised I must be away.

I cant tell you how much I appreciate your having sent me something belonging to Freddy, and I shall always value the owl that he was fond of.

Thank you so very much.

With kindest remembrance to you and Mr. Longman,

Yours v. sincerely,
Godfrey Thomas

War Memorial, Harrow School

There were 644 Old Harrovians killed in the Great War. A permanent memorial building was erected at the school and opened in 1926. The first meeting called to begin planning for this memorial was in 1917. Freddy's name is recorded amongst his school colleagues. His father contributed £50 towards the cost.

Pembroke College, Cambridge

A memorial along the walls of the Old Court outside the college chapel was erected to commemorate past students who had lost their lives in conflict. Freddy Longman is remembered here amongst hundreds of other fellow students.

Commonwealth War Graves Commission

The Le Touret Memorial lies between Lille and Bethune in northern France and commemorates over 13,400 British soldiers who were killed in this area of the Western Front from the beginning of October 1914 to the eve of the Battle of Loos in late September 1915 and who have no known grave. The Memorial takes the form of a loggia surrounding an open rectangular court. The names are listed on panels set into the walls of the court and the gallery, arranged by regiment, rank and alphabetically by surname within the rank. The memorial was designed by John Reginald Truelove, who had served as an officer with the London Regiment and unveiled by the British ambassador to France, Lord Tyrrell, on 22nd March 1930. Freddy's name can be found inscribed on panel six.

The War Memorial at Pembroke College, Cambridge

Children's Chapel, St Mary's Church, Braughing, Hertfordshire

Following the death of Freddy's father in 1934, Mrs Longman arranged for the creation of a Children's chapel beneath the stained glass window dedicated to her son.

On 3rd April 1936 the Hertfordshire Mercury published details of a special service conducted by the Bishop of Bedford:

A confirmation and dedication service conducted by the Bishop of Bedford was held at St. Mary's, Braughing on Friday [26 March]. Sixty-seven children from Braughing, Crofton Grange [school], Albury, Barley, Buntingford, Cottered, and Great Hormead were confirmed.

The children's chapel dedicated by the Bishop, is under the window by R. Anning Bell, A.R.A., erected in memory of Frederick Longman, and is part of the memorial.

A Della Robbia plaque of the Holy Family hangs in the centre of the oak-panelled chapel, over a carved altar table. On the floor stand two Florentine vases. Other ornaments are Florentine candlesticks, a Tudor altar cushion worked in silver and gold thread, a Persian rug in front of the altar, and hassocks of mosaic tapestry.

Books and pictures for the children are kept on an oak chest.

The design and arrangements concerning the chapel have been carried out under Mr Hugh Easton.

Dame Joan Evans

Freddy was remembered by his aunt Joan Evans, his mother's half sister in her autobiography, *Prelude & Fugue,* published in 1964. Joan was three years younger than Freddy and recalled the following (p 72):

'The autumn of 1914 was in any case inevitably a time of sadness. The friendliest of my nephews, who under the compulsion of a premonition of war had given up scientific work to join the Royal Fusiliers a year or two before, was killed in France early in the term; a friend whom I might well have married was killed a few days later; and I felt the senseless destruction of Rheims as an acute personal loss......'

Freddy's father Charles died in 1934, leaving his mother Harriet to sort out the estate. She sold Upp Hall and moved out. In preparation for moving house, she hired a photographer to take a series of photographs of the house and grounds. One such photograph was of Freddy's bedroom, left untouched since he left home twenty years before.

Although prematurely taken from this world, Freddy is far from forgotten.

We shall remember

Children's Chapel created by Mrs Harriet Longman in 1936

Freddy's bedroom at Upp Hall taken in 1934

ACKNOWLEDGEMENTS

First and foremost, my sincere thanks and gratitude go to Mrs Mary Harley, niece of Frederick Longman for access to the family archives including Freddy's letters and personal diary as well as family photographs and various memorabilia that bring this story alive.

I would also like to express my gratitude to the Heritage Hub of the University of Hertfordshire for their kind generosity in awarding a grant to assist with publication costs.

Finally, my thanks go to Mary Nokes, Clive Marshall and Madeline Marshall for their valued assistance and expertise in helping to bring this project to publication.

Mary Harley and Peter Boylan taken in May 2013 in Scotland

Various sources of information have been used in the preparation of this book. The main sources are listed below:

HALS (Hertfordshire Archives and Local Studies)

National Archives for access to military records relating to Lieutenant Frederick Longman and the Royal Fusiliers

Hertfordshire Mercury who recorded various events relating to the Great War as it affected Braughing

St Mary's Church, Braughing – *Golden Book of Braughing*

Harrow School Archives and access to *The Harrovian* magazine

Pembroke College, Cambridge Archives

H. C. O'Neill, *The Royal Fusiliers in the Great War,* William Heineman, 1922

Dame Joan Evans, *Prelude & Fugue*, Museum Press, 1964

D. S. Higgins, *The Private Diaries of Sir Henry Rider Haggard 1914-1925,* Cassell, 1980

Harrow School, *Harrow Memorials of the Great War Volume 1,* 1918

Andrew Lang, *The Animal Story Book,* Longmans Green & Co 1896

Peter Boylan